The Power of The A3s

The Power of
The A3s

Gavin Morrison

OPC
Oxford Publishing Co

Half title:
No 60104 *Solario* had the dubious honour of being the first 'A3' to be withdrawn in December 1959, despite having undergone a classified and non-classified repair earlier in the year. It received a double chimney in April 1959, but never carried deflectors. It is seen here leaving Stoke Tunnel, heading a down express on 2 August 1958 during its period allocated to Doncaster. *Gavin Morrison*

Frontispiece:
Displaying a Grantham shedplate, No 60065 *Knight of Thistle* leaves Newcastle Central's Platform 9 at the head of the up 'Heart of Midlothian' on 13 April 1960. A strong wind and some slipping have combined to produce an impressive exhaust effect. *I. S. Carr*

Title page:
In what appears to be an official works picture, No 2743 (later No 60089) *Felstead* poses for the photographer. This was the first new 'A3', and was built at Doncaster in August 1928. It is fitted with a Type 94 HP boiler and a corridor tender. *Ian Allan Library*

Bibliography
Railway Correspondence and Travel Society, *Locomotives of the LNER, Part 2A*
Yeadon's Register of LNER Locomotives, Volume 1

Printed by Ian Allan Printing Ltd, Hersham, Surrey KT12 4RG.

Code: 0208/A3

Introduction

Probably everything that there is to know about the 'A3s' has already appeared in print before, but as far as I am aware, as with other classes in the 'Power' series, this will be the first book containing around 250 pictures of the class, and showing every locomotive. It is intended to be a photographic record, wherein I think I have managed to illustrate every livery and most of the features that affected the appearance of the engines.

The book begins with a short section showing the locomotives when they were 'A1s', as I felt it would be incomplete without it, and I wanted to illustrate somewhere in the book the original 'A1' *Great Northern* before it was rebuilt.

The very high profile that the 'A3s' have enjoyed over the years must be largely due to their association with the most famous train in the world, the 'Flying Scotsman', and the locomotive named after it. I am not suggesting that this makes the 'A3s' the most famous class in the world, but they must be very high on that list for being the best-known in this country.

When the original 'A1' *Great Northern* appeared in 1922, a new era started. It was the second Pacific to be built in Britain, after the Great Western's *The Great Bear*, and it achieved Sir Nigel Gresley's aims of having a locomotive capable of hauling a 600-ton train at 70mph on the level, and climbing gradients such as Stoke Bank at 45mph with similar loads, not that these loads were an everyday requirement. Another reason for the fame of the class, and of No 4472 *Flying Scotsman* in particular, was that it was the first in the country to achieve a fully authenticated 100mph, on 30 November 1934.

The famous Wembley exhibition of 1925, when *Flying Scotsman* was exhibited with a Great Western 'Castle', had surprising repercussions for the future of the 'A1' class, as it was decided to run comparative trials between the two classes on the Great Western main line to Plymouth and on the East Coast main line, and it has to be said that in terms of fuel economy the Gresley design did not show up well against the 'Castle'. The result was that Doncaster decided to modify No 4480 *Enterprise* by increasing the boiler pressure from 180psi to 220psi, and fitting new 20in-diameter cylinders, thus increasing the tractive effort. Further tests were carried out on No 2544 *Lemberg* with the cylinder diameter reduced to 19in. The final outcome of these tests was that coal consumption figures were compared, and the modified locomotives were reclassified as 'A3s'.

The full details about these tests and modifications are described in great detail, as are all other matters regarding the 'A1s' and 'A3s', in the Railway Correspondence &

Travel Society's publication *Locomotives of the LNER, Part 2A*. This excellent book, now sadly out of print, together with *Yeadon's Register of LNER Locomotives, Part 1*, will provide all the technical information about the 'A3s' and their background, and it is from these fine books that most of the information given in the captions has been gained.

In the late 1930s the order was given that the whole of the 'A1' class was to be modified to 'A3' specifications, and 27 new locomotives were constructed as 'A3s'. The process of complete conversion of the class took more than 20 years, although no doubt it would have been done much more quickly had it not been for World War 2.

The locomotives in both forms put in excellent work and the LNER Publicity Department certainly pulled off a coup by naming them after racehorses. But like racehorses they performed at their best when they received top-class care or maintenance, and with the outbreak of the war maintenance standards fell, coal quality deteriorated, and the conjugated valve gear in particular did not like this treatment. Consequently the performance deteriorated rapidly, and after the war it was felt in many quarters that the locomotives had had their day, especially with the appearance of the new 'A1s' and 'A2s'.

This sorry state of affairs continued in the immediate postwar years, but gradually the maintenance standards improved at the main sheds, and Haymarket adopted the principle of allocating engines to individual drivers, while others tried to keep engines on regular workings, so the class gradually regained their former capabilities. In 1958 it was decided to fit the entire class with the Kylchap double blastpipe. The transformation of the locomotives was excellent, making them the equal in terms of performance to the English Electric Class 40 diesel-electrics that in due course appeared to replace them. Why this seemed to come as such a surprise is hard to understand, as all experimenting had been done with No 2751 (later 60097) *Humorist* 20 years earlier, and it had always been regarded as a vastly superior performer to the rest of the class. I have never read any explanation for the delay, which applied equally well to the famous Class A4s.

The other problem with the class after the fitting of the double chimneys was drifting smoke, and again this is reported to have been solved on No 60097 *Humorist*, which ran with deflectors of various types. Eventually the German trough-type deflectors started to be fitted, the first recipient being No 60049 *Galtee More* as late as October 1960, so it is not surprising that 22 members of the class never received that type of deflector.

By 1961 the Eastern Region was blessed with around

200 Pacifics, and the 'A3s' were better than they had ever been, but of course this was just as the famous 'Deltics' and Brush Class 47s were starting to appear. This glorious swan-song for the class was therefore short-lived on East Coast main line duties; the first withdrawal came in November 1961 with No 60102 *Sir Frederick Banbury* after almost 40 years' service and around 2 million miles.

The withdrawals came thick and fast in the next few years, although Doncaster continued to give general overhauls as late as 1963, but many that received them did little work thereafter. The end finally came in January 1966 when No 60052 *Prince Palatine* was withdrawn. It had, together with about two or three others, finished its days in the Scottish Region, mainly working freight trains over the Waverley route.

My happiest memories of the class are during the short period when they were allocated to Leeds Holbeck for working the Scottish expresses over the Settle & Carlisle line, and in spite of the fact that few of them were in very good condition during their brief stay, the Midland men certainly appreciated their free steaming and their relatively comfortable cabs and smooth riding compared to the equally capable but less comfortable 'Rebuilt Scots' that they had driven for the previous 17 years.

The class remained intact except for the almost complete destruction of No 2744 *Grand Parade* in the Castlecary accident of 1937, although it was rebuilt, thus keeping the class numerically complete.

Fortunately, thanks to Alan Pegler, No 4472 (60103) *Flying Scotsman* is still with us, and has now been in preservation for almost 40 years, nearly as long as its main-line career. It has become the most widely travelled locomotive in this country, not to mention its visit to the United States, and it has provided pleasure to millions of people over the years. Nor must we forget the owners of the locomotive, who over the years have overcome the many difficulties, especially the financial ones, in keeping it running. While the locomotive with its double chimney can never be as exciting to hear as when it had a single chimney, or indeed as beautiful to look at, it must be acknowledged that its performance is vastly superior.

Finally, my thanks to all the photographers whose work appears in this book, especially those who helped me in providing pictures of the few members of the class that seemed particularly camera-shy.

Gavin Morrison
2002

Background to the 'A3s'

This section is intended to illustrate the background to the 'A3s', of which 27 were constructed new while 52 were converted from 'A1s' over a period of just over 21 years, starting with No 4480 *Enterprise* in July 1927 and ending with No 68 *Sir Visto* (by then designated Class A10) in December 1948. There was also of course No 1470 (GNR number), later No 4470, *Great Northern*, which was chosen by Thompson as a prototype for the 'A1s', and was never converted to an 'A3'.

Above:
Great Northern is shown in its original condition, painted in Great Northern livery as it was completed in April 1922 prior to the Grouping. It was built to the Great Northern loading gauge with high roof and tall chimney, and was only the second Pacific to be built for a British company, 14 years after the first, the Great Western's *The Great Bear*. *Ian Allan Library*

Left:
The fireman looks relaxed as No 1471 E *Sir Frederick Banbury* heads north in fine style. The picture is not dated, but the locomotive worked its first train out of King's Cross on 24 July 1922, and on 3 September worked a 20-coach 600-ton test train to Grantham in 121 minutes for the 105 miles. *Ian Allan Library*

Left:
Flying Scotsman was the first 'A1' to be completed at Doncaster Works after the Grouping, in February 1923, when it emerged with the LNER crest on the cabside, and 'LNER' and '4472' on the tender. It was exhibited at Wembley as part of the 1924 Empire Exhibition, when it was named, and again in 1925 at the Centenary of British Railways Exhibition. It was fitted with special polished brass beading to the coupled wheel splashers. No 4472 is seen here on the turntable at Grantham in 1927. *T. G. Hepburn*

Above:
After the Wembley Empire Exhibition it was decided to send Great Western No 4079 *Pendennis Castle* for trials on the East Coast main line, to compare its performance against an 'A1'. No 4475 *Flying Fox* was chosen to represent the latter class, but ran hot and was substituted by No 2545 *Diamond Jubilee*. While *Great Northern* had achieved Sir Nigel Gresley's target of being able to haul a 600-ton express to the schedules required, the 'A1s' did not compare well with the 'Castle' in terms of coal economy, burning 3.7lb per mile more than the 'Castle'. This resulted in alterations to the valve gear of the 'A1s' and ultimately to a higher boiler pressure, thereby creating what became the 'A3s'. *Pendennis Castle* is shown alongside *Flying Fox* on King's Cross shed. *Ian Allan Library*

Above:
A very early picture (probably taken in 1923) of No 1476 carrying 'L&NER' on the tender and prior to being named *Royal Lancer* and receiving the number 4476. *Ian Allan Library*

Above:
A superb picture of No 4473 *Solario* storming past Greenwood on the down 4pm train from King's Cross on 14 September 1934, when it was allocated to King's Cross shed.
E. R. Wethersett

Right:
Main-line sights don't come much better than an LNER apple green 'A1' at the head of a Pullman train. No 4477 *Gay Crusader* is seen near New Southgate on 10 September 1938 on the down 'Yorkshire Pullman'. It was allocated to Doncaster at this time.
E. R. Wethersett

Left:
It must be many years since *Flying Scotsman* headed a train in this external condition, but I have included this picture just to show that it didn't always look immaculate. It is passing New Southgate on 20 July 1946, when it was classified as an 'A10'. *E. R. Wethersett*

Below:
Melton became No 44 before it was rebuilt as an 'A3' in September 1947, when it received the LNER apple green livery. This picture was taken when it was still in black livery and shows it at the head of a down Leeds express. *E. R. Wethersett*

Above:
Windsor Lad with the new-type non-corridor tender it retained for its entire career. Except for around 10 weeks in its 27 years of service, it was always a Haymarket engine. *Ian Allan Library*

Centre right:
In the usual immaculate Haymarket shed condition, *Windsor Lad* is seen ready to leave Edinburgh Waverley for Perth in the early 1950s. *Eric Treacy*

2500/60035 *Windsor Lad*

Built as 'A3'

Entered traffic	10 July 1934
Renumbered	35 (December 1946); 60035 (July 1948)
Liveries	LNER green when new
	Black April 1942
	LNER green September 1947
	BR blue January 1950
	BR green August 1951
Allocations	New to Haymarket
	Aberdeen 28 March 1937
	Haymarket 4 April 1937
	Carlisle Canal 23 April 1961
	Haymarket 28 August 1961
Withdrawn	4 September 1961; at Doncaster Works on that date for repair, but condemned

Lower right:
Now fitted with the double chimney, which it received in January 1959, *Windsor Lad* heads a Newcastle-Edinburgh train near Burnmouth on 6 June 1960. It never received the trough-type smoke deflectors. *R. Leslie*

2501/60036 *Colombo*

Built as 'A3'	
Entered traffic	9 July 1934
Renumbered	36 (1 December 1946);
	60036 (23 July 1948)
Liveries	LNER green when new
	Black August 1942
	LNER green April 1947
	Purple July 1948
	BR blue July 1949
	BR green December 1951
Allocations	New to Gateshead
	York 9 December 1939
	Heaton 28 March 1943
	Gateshead 3 November 1945
	King's Cross 1 August 1947
	Gateshead 9 September 1947
	Neville Hill 6 February 1949
	Copley Hill 11 June 1961
	Ardsley 10 September 1961
	Gateshead 16 June 1963
	Darlington 15 December 1963
Withdrawn	23 November 1964; scrapped at
	A. Draper, Hull, January 1965

Above:
Colombo must have made a very fine sight in its LNER apple green livery as it passed Prestonpans on the 8.30am Darlington to Edinburgh train on 23 April 1948. *E. R. Wethersett*

Above:
Double-headed Pacifics on the East Coast main line were fairly rare, but on 23 February 1954 the 10.05am Newcastle-Holloway empty stock working produced the impressive combination of *Colombo* and Class A2 No 60516 *Hycilla*. The train is seen near Thirsk. *J. W. Hague*

Above:

With its East Coast main line duties having been taken over by diesels, *Colombo*, although still allocated to Neville Hill shed, was often borrowed by Holbeck at this time to work over the Settle & Carlisle line on the 'Waverley' and 'Thames-Clyde' expresses. Complete with headboard, it is shown drifting past Bingley Junction, Shipley, on the up working on 10 May 1961. The locomotive spent over 12 years at Neville Hill, most of its time working the 'North Briton' and 'Queen of Scots' expresses between Leeds and Newcastle. The locomotive was involved in an accident at York station in the late 1950s when it failed to stop at the buffers. There is an interesting selection of cars in the background that would now be classics! *Gavin Morrison*

Above:

Colombo received its trough deflectors in July 1962, at its last general overhaul. On 21 December 1962 it is still looking in good external condition as it arrives at Leeds with a relief train from Sunderland to Manchester. It was allocated to Ardsley shed at the time, where there was probably very little work for it by this date. *J. M. Rayner*

2502/60037 *Hyperion*

Built as 'A3'	
Entered traffic	25 July 1934
Renumbered	37 (25 August 1946);
	60037 (25 October 1948)
Liveries	LNER green when new
	Black January 1943
	LNER green July 1947
	BR blue June 1950
	BR green March 1952
Allocations	New to Haymarket
	St Margarets 6 March 1938
	Haymarket 15 March 1939
	Carlisle 7 February 1954
	Haymarket 8 March 1954
	St Margarets
	6 November 1961
Withdrawn	12 December 1963; scrapped
	at Arnott Young, Carmyle,
	June 1964

Above:

Only one month after receiving a general overhaul, when it was repainted in LNER apple green after wartime black, *Hyperion* is climbing along the coast from Berwick towards Burnmouth on the 9.50am from King's Cross on 25 August 1947. The locomotive spent most of its working career at Haymarket, and was seldom seen south of Newcastle except when visiting Doncaster Works for overhaul. *E. R. Wethersett*

Below:

The station clock shows 11.12am on 22 August 1947, which probably indicates that *Hyperion* is heading the 10am from Edinburgh Waverley to Glasgow Queen Street. It is about to descend the steep 1 in 41 Cowlairs Bank, and the ex-North British Class N15s in the background will be acting as bankers. *E. R. Wethersett*

Above:
Mundane work for an 'A3' Pacific: *Hyperion* is near the border just north of Berwick as it heads north on a coal train on 25 July 1952. In August 1941 the locomotive received an original Great Northern tender with coal rails, which remained with the locomotive until withdrawal. *E. R. Wethersett*

Below:
After its regular main-line duties had been taken over by diesels at Haymarket, *Hyperion* moved to St Margarets shed. Occasionally the Pacifics at the shed at this time were used on Edinburgh-Leeds expresses over the Waverley and Settle & Carlisle lines, when Class 45 'Peaks' failed. This was obviously how No 60037 had arrived on Holbeck shed on 19 July 1962. It received its double chimney in October 1958 and the trough deflectors during May 1962. *Gavin Morrison*

2503/60038 *Firdaussi*

Built as 'A3'	
Entered traffic	11 August 1934
Renumbered	38 (27 October 1946);
	60038 (10 June 1948)
Liveries	LNER green when new
	Black April 1942
	LNER green March 1947
	BR blue January 1950
	BR green September 1951
Allocations	New to Gateshead
	Heaton 30 September 1939
	Gateshead 10 November 1939
	Heaton 4 January 1943
	Darlington 22 February 1953
	Gateshead 30 August 1953
	Darlington 19 August 1956
	Gateshead 24 February 1957
	Holbeck (Leeds)
	21 February 1960
	Neville Hill 16 June 1963
Withdrawn	18 November 1963; cut up
	at Darlington Works,
	31 December 1963

Upper left:
Firdaussi is approaching Penmanshiel Tunnel (now closed after it collapsed in April 1979) at the top of the 1 in 96 Cockburnspath Bank with an up meat train for south of the border on 23 May 1957. *C. J. B. Sanderson*

Centre left:
During their short spell allocated to Leeds Holbeck shed, it was very unusual to see an 'A3' being double-headed. On 16 July 1960 the up 'Thames-Clyde Express' receives a helping hand from Kingmoor-allocated Stanier Class 5 No 44886. The train is shown passing Ais Gill summit but the reason for the double-heading is not known. *Gavin Morrison*

Lower left:
Firdaussi went to Doncaster Works for its last general overhaul in April 1961. In spite of the fact that the Class 45 'Peaks' had arrived at Holbeck to work the Scottish expresses by this date, No 60038 returned to the shed at the beginning of June 1961 and remained there long after all the others had departed. It was primarily used on the 10.35am Leeds-Glasgow St Enoch train, returning during the night with the up sleeper. On 7 September 1962 it was unusually diagrammed for an up freight, and is seen passing Wortley Junction, Leeds. *Gavin Morrison*

2504/60039 Sandwich

Built as 'A3'	
Entered traffic	9 September 1934
Renumbered	39 (8 July 1946);
	60039 (9 July 1948)
Liveries	LNER green when new
	Black September 1942
	LNER green September 1946
	BR blue March 1950
	BR green October 1951
Allocations	New to Gateshead
	Doncaster 30 November 1935
	King's Cross 6 March 1939
	Grantham 9 December 1941
	King's Cross 4 June 1950
	Grantham 9 September 1951
	Leicester Central 7 October 1956
	King's Cross 7 April 1957
Withdrawn	14 March 1963; to Doncaster Works
	for cutting up, 5 April 1963

Below:
Sandwich went new to the North East, but was exchanged for Class A4 *Silver King* so that Gateshead had an 'A4' to cover for the 'Silver Jubilee' in case of an emergency. While allocated to Doncaster, *Sandwich* is seen in charge of the up 'Yorkshire Pullman' near Potters Bar on 27 March 1937. It is attached to a non-corridor tender, which it retained until withdrawal. *E. R. Wethersett*

Bottom:
This undated picture, probably taken around 1949, shows *Sandwich* in LNER green but carrying British Railways number 60039 in the yard outside King's Cross awaiting its next duty. *Ian Allan Library*

Left:
Another fine picture of *Sandwich* heading the 'Yorkshire Pullman', this time the down train on 11 July 1958, between the tunnels at Welwyn. It was a King's Cross-allocated locomotive at the time, where it remained until withdrawal. *E. R. Wethersett*

Below:
Sandwich received its double chimney in July 1959 and nearly two years later, in June 1961 during a visit to Doncaster Works, had the trough deflectors fitted. It is in Doncaster Works on 29 September 1962 in immaculate condition for its last casual light repair. *Gavin Morrison*

Upper right:
Cameronian bursts out of Welwyn Tunnel at the head of an up express. It swapped its original new-type non-corridor tender for the Great Northern type with coal rails, as seen here, during November 1936. The picture was taken on 11 April 1939.
E. R. Wethersett

Centre right:
Possibly due to being diverted via Bishop Auckland, the 4.30pm Newcastle-Leeds train on 29 July 1962 is double-headed by *Cameronian* and Class V2 2-6-2 No 60939, and is seen near Brancepeth. It received its double chimney in October 1959 and the trough deflectors in March 1962. *V. Wake*

2505/60040 *Cameronian*

Built as 'A3'	
Entered traffic	27 October 1934
Renumbered	575 (17 March 1946); 40 (19 May 1946); 60040 (31 August 1948)
Liveries	LNER green when new Black November 1942 LNER green March 1947 BR blue December 1949 BR green May 1952
Allocations	New to Haymarket Gateshead 16 November 1936 York 9 December 1939 Heaton 28 March 1943 Shared by Gateshead and Darlington 3 November 1945 Heaton 9 December 1962 Gateshead 16 June 1963
Withdrawn	6 July 1964; to Hughes Bolckow, North Blyth, for scrap, September 1964

Lower right:
In less than immaculate condition, and when allocated to Heaton, *Cameronian* is dead on Doncaster shed on 24 March 1963. *Gavin Morrison*

Left:
Salmon Trout is shown in the purple/blue livery it received during a works visit in May 1948. This experimental livery was applied to eight of the class, and *Salmon Trout* also had the cylinder casing lined in red and cream, which varied from the others. Between October 1935 and January 1937 *Salmon Trout* was attached to a corridor tender, but this was changed for the Great Northern type for the rest of its career. It is shown here climbing to Grantshouse on an up express on 13 August 1949, with at least 13 coaches behind the tender. The locomotive carried four different liveries in less than five years, which even by modern-day standards seems excessive.
E. R. Wethersett

2506/60041 *Salmon Trout*

Built as 'A3'
Entered traffic 19 December 1934
Renumbered 41 (7 July 1946);
60041 (26 November 1948)
Liveries LNER green when new
Black May 1942
LNER green May 1947
Purple May 1948
BR blue July 1950
BR green February 1952
Allocations New to Haymarket
St Margarets 13 July 1960
Withdrawn 4 December 1965; sold to
Arnott Young, Carmyle, for
scrap, September 1966

Centre right:
In typically immaculate Haymarket condition, this fine picture shows *Salmon Trout* passing its home depot of Haymarket, where it was allocated for more than 25 years. It is heading an Edinburgh Waverley-Glasgow Queen Street express on 13 September 1953, having received a general repair four months earlier.
J. Robertson

Lower right:
Salmon Trout is seen at Hawick at the head of a Stephenson Locomotive Society special heading south in April 1963. The locomotive had undergone a general repair at Doncaster in January of that year, which was probably why it was the penultimate member of the class to remain in service. It received the double chimney in July 1959, but it was another 3½ years before the deflectors were fitted. *Ian Allan Library*

2507/60042 *Singapore*

Built as 'A3'

Entered traffic	1 December 1934
Renumbered	42 (10 November 1946); 60042 (9 April 1948)
Liveries	LNER green when new
	Black August 1943
	LNER green June 1947
	BR blue April 1950
	BR green August 1951
Allocations	New to Gateshead
	Neville Hill 27 September 1945
	Gateshead and Darlington 6 May 1946
	Heaton 9 September 1962
	Aberdeen 7 April 1963
	St Margarets 27 October 1963
Withdrawn	13 July 1964; sold to Arnott Young, Carmyle, for scrap, October 1964

Above:
This fine portrait of *Singapore* is undated, but was probably taken around 1936 before it received a GNR-type tender with coal rails. It received a new-type non-corridor tender between September 1941 and August 1943, but it is unlikely that the locomotive would have been in so clean a condition during the war. It is at the head of a stopping train about to leave Peterborough. *T. G. Hepburn*

Above:
Singapore passes Grove Road at Retford and starts the 1 in 178/200 climb to the 57yd long Askham Tunnel, 3½ miles to the south, with an up express in 1956. *D. Penney*

2507/60042 *Singapore*

Left:
Three enthusiasts observe the passing of *Singapore* at the site of Great Ponton station, which closed to passenger traffic on 15 September 1958. No 60042 is heading a down express on 17 June 1961, when the goods yard was still open, although this ceased operations on 29 April 1963. The locomotive had received its double chimney in September 1958, but it was to be another 15 months before the deflectors were fitted. *Gavin Morrison*

Below:
Singapore had received its last general overhaul only one month earlier, in September 1962, when it was photographed at Leeds Central waiting to leave with the up 'White Rose' on 2 October 1962. The Pullman coaches on the left belong to the down 'Queen of Scots', headed by a 'Deltic'. The locomotive was attached to a new-type tender twice during its career, but from August 1943 it ran with a GNR type with coal rails. It received the trough deflectors during its last overhaul, and the double chimney four years earlier. Although it shows a 52A Gateshead shedplate, it had, according to the records, been transferred to Heaton on 9 September 1962. It moved to Scotland in April 1963, and worked alongside the 'A4s' on the Aberdeen-Glasgow services. *Gavin Morrison*

Above:
Brown Jack pulls away from Perth with seven coaches forming an up stopping train to Edinburgh on 24 June 1957, while a Stanier Class 5 heads towards the station. No 60043 ran with new-type non-corridor and streamlined non-corridor tenders until May 1938, when a GNR type with coal rails was attached. It went into Doncaster for a general repair about six weeks after this picture was taken, which may explain why it was on stopping train duties. *Brown Jack* was the last 'A3' to be built.
Brian E. Morrison

2508/60043 *Brown Jack*

Built as 'A3'	
Entered traffic	9 February 1935
Renumbered	43 (23 August 1946);
	60043 (11 August 1948)
Liveries	LNER green when new
	Black June 1942
	LNER green June 1947
	BR blue April 1950
	BR green August 1951
Allocations	New to Haymarket
	St Margarets
	6 November 1961
Withdrawn	14 May 1964; sold to
	Motherwell Machinery
	Scrap Co, Wishaw, July 1964

Right:
Brown Jack received a double chimney in February 1959, and deflectors three years later. In this picture it is crossing the viaduct on the approaches to Newcastle Central with an up Anglo-Scottish car carrier on 31 August 1960. Note the reversed headboard below the chimney.
C. P. Walker

Left:
Apart from the 2½ years spent working on the Great Central, *Melton* spent all its time as an 'A3' allocated to ex-Great Northern main-line sheds. It must have presented a fine sight in its LNER green livery with unshaded Gill Sans lettering as it headed an up Newcastle-King's Cross express at Stevenage on 3 July 1948. *E. R. Wethersett*

2543/60044 *Melton*

Built new as 'A1'	June 1924; to traffic as 'A3' 18 September 1947
Renumbered	44 (September 1946); 60044 (August 1949)
Liveries (as 'A3')	LNER green September 1947 BR blue August 1949 BR green December 1952
Allocations (as 'A3')	New England 18 September 1947 Grantham 9 November 1947 Copley Hill 23 April 1950 Doncaster 9 September 1951 Leicester Central 15 November 1953 Neasden 27 March 1955 King's Cross 25 March 1956 Grantham 16 September 1956 King's Cross 7 April 1957
Withdrawn	16 June 1963; to Doncaster Works for scrapping, 25 November 1963

Left:
At the south end of Grantham station *Melton* prepares to leave with the up 10.20am Saltburn-King's Cross train on 4 August 1957. *R. A. Panting*

Left:
Melton is seen in Doncaster Works after a casual light repair on 29 September 1962. It had received the double chimney in June 1959 and the deflectors in August 1961. Compared to the two earlier pictures it will be noted that it is now carrying a boiler with a 'banjo'-type steam-collecting dome, which was fitted during an overhaul in October 1959. *Gavin Morrison*

Above:

Just under two years since being rebuilt as an 'A3', *Lemberg* makes a fine sight storming along the East Coast main line near Potters Bar on 2 September 1929. *Lemberg* was the second 'A1' to be rebuilt as an 'A3', and in February 1928 it was selected, together with 'A1' No 4473 *Solario*, to carry out comparative trials on the 11.04am Doncaster-King's Cross service and the 4pm return. *Solario* had been fitted with long-travel valves, and the conclusion of the trials was that there was little difference between the locomotives, and both were capable of carrying out the duties allocated to them on the main line. It must be mentioned that *Lemberg* suffered from the relief valves on the cylinders blowing, and on one day the piston glands were also blowing, which no doubt had an adverse effect on its performance. *E. R. Wethersett*

2544/60045 *Lemberg*

Built new as 'A1'	July 1924; entered traffic as 'A3' 3 December 1927
Renumbered	45 (September 1946); 60045 (June 1948)
Liveries (as 'A3')	LNER green December 1927 Black December 1942 LNER green September 1947 BR purple June 1948 BR blue November 1950 BR green April 1952
Allocations (as 'A3')	Doncaster 3 December 1927 Reallocated 16 times between Gateshead, Heaton and Darlington 6 January 1937- 15 December 1963
Withdrawn	23 November 1964; sold to A. Draper, Hull, for scrap, January 1965

Below:

In fine external condition *Lemberg* has just started to descend Stoke Bank with an up Glasgow Queen Street-King's Cross express on 30 July 1951, during its 14-year period allocated to Gateshead shed. It had received a brand-new boiler in November 1950 during a general overhaul.
E. R. Wethersett

Above:

The evening shadows are lengthening on *Lemberg* as it stands at the south end of Darlington shed on what is now known as 'Thunderbird' duties. Darlington used to receive Pacifics from Gateshead or Heaton sheds for these stand-by duties, and they usually seemed to get changed about every four months. *Gavin Morrison*

Below:

Lemberg is now shown in its final form on Doncaster shed on 7 April 1963, once again looking in fine external condition. At this date, as the shedplate shows, it was again a stand-by locomotive at Darlington. The double chimney was fitted in October 1959 and the deflectors in November 1962. *Gavin Morrison*

Right:
Diamond Jubilee makes a fine sight as it passes Eaton Wood near Retford with an up express in 1957 when it was allocated to Doncaster. *D. Penney*

2545/60046 *Diamond Jubilee*

Built new as 'A1'	August 1924; entered traffic as 'A3' 23 August 1941
Renumbered	46 (13 July 1946); 60046 (5 August 1949)
Liveries (as 'A3')	LNER green August 1941 Black March 1943 LNER green November 1947 BR blue August 1949 BR green October 1952
Allocations (as 'A3')	Grantham 23 August 1941 Copley Hill 30 September 1943 King's Cross 8 December 1944 Copley Hill 30 May 1948 Doncaster 9 September 1951 Grantham 14 June 1959 New England 9 September 1962 Grantham 21 April 1963
Withdrawn	16 June 1963; cut up at Doncaster Works, 20 August 1963

Centre right:
The shortage of cleaners at Grantham at this time must have been acute, as *Diamond Jubilee* presents a sorry sight as it passes Holbeck High Level on 28 August 1961 with the up 11.37am train to King's Cross. The double chimney was fitted during a general overhaul in August 1958, and the locomotive ran with a streamlined non-corridor tender from June 1937. *Gavin Morrison*

Lower right:
Diamond Jubilee is seen in its final form on Grantham shed during July 1962, the deflectors having been fitted in the previous December. *K. R. Pirt*

2546/60047 *Donovan*

Built new as 'A1'	August 1924; entered traffic as 'A3' 9 January 1948
Renumbered	47 (September 1946); 60047 (8 May 1948)
Liveries (as 'A3')	LNER green January 1948 BR blue August 1949 BR green October 1952
Allocations (as 'A3')	King's Cross 9 January1948 Doncaster 4 June 1950 King's Cross 7 January1951 Grantham 9 September 1951 King's Cross 20 June 1954 Grantham 17 October 1954 New England 9 September 1962
Withdrawn	8 April 1963; to Doncaster Works for scrapping, 19 June 1963

Above:
I am afraid there are no details of this fine picture of *Donovan* heading a down express at the southern end of the East Coast main line with a wide variety of coaching stock — the first two appear to be a suburban articulated pair. The date would be the early 1950s. *Ian Allan Library*

Above:
Grantham shed in its latter years seemed to be very short of cleaners, and the external condition of *Donovan* on 26 June 1960 was fairly normal. It had a casual light repair one month earlier at Doncaster, but had received its double chimney in July 1959. It is seen pulling away from York past the racecourse station on a hot summer's day. *Gavin Morrison*

Left:
Donovan is seen here at its then home shed of Grantham in August 1962, in its final condition and looking much cleaner than in the previous picture. *K. R. Pirt*

A powerful picture of *Doncaster* heading an express near Lea in 1957, having been diverted off the East Coast main line via Doncaster, Gainsborough and Lincoln. *D. Penney*

2547/60048 *Doncaster*

Built new as 'A1'	August 1924; entered traffic as 'A3' 16 May 1946
Renumbered	48 (16 May 1946); 60048 (11 November 1948)
Liveries (as 'A3')	Black May 1946 LNER green June 1947 BR blue September 1950 BR green September 1952
Allocations (as 'A3')	Doncaster 16 May 1946 Leicester Central 6 February 1949 Doncaster 15 November 1953 King's Cross 8 June 1958 Doncaster 25 January 1959 Grantham 8 February 1959 New England 9 September 1962 Grantham 21 April 1963
Withdrawn	8 September 1963; to Doncaster Works for scrapping, 19 September 1963

Right:
Doncaster puts on a fine exhaust as it climbs past Copley Hill shed at Leeds with the up 12.30pm Leeds Central to King's Cross express. It is carrying the wing deflectors that were fitted in November 1959 to four members of the class, but which were replaced in December 1961.
Gavin Morrison

Left:
This is *Doncaster* in its final form after its last general repair at 'The Plant'. It is seen at Copley Hill shed at Leeds on 24 April 1962. Note the lower position of the front number, and that the locomotive had received a new-type non-corridor tender during this overhaul. *Gavin Morrison*

2548/60049 *Galtee More*

Built as 'A1'	September 1924; entered traffic as 'A3' 13 October 1945
Renumbered	517 (25 April 1946); 49 (14 July 1946); 60049 (24 June 1948)
Liveries (as 'A3')	Black October 1945 LNER green December 1946 BR blue August 1950 BR green July 1952
Allocations (as 'A3')	Doncaster 13 October 1945 Leicester Central 6 February 1949 King's Cross 26 June 1955 Leicester Central 23 October 1955 Grantham 15 September 1957
Withdrawn	29 December 1962; to Doncaster Works for cutting up, 4 April 1963

Above:
A powerful picture of *Galtee More* overflowing the tender on Charwelton troughs at the head of the 'South Yorkshireman'. Unfortunately there are no details for this picture, but it was obviously taken before the locomotive left the Great Central shed in 1957. It probably spent more time on the Great Central than any other 'A3'. *Ian Allan Library*

Centre left:
Galtee More is ready for its next duty on Grantham shed in June 1959, three months after the fitting of the double chimney. It ran with a Great Northern-type tender during its entire career. *K. R. Pirt*

Below:
Galtee More is seen at Doncaster Works, which it had entered for the last time three days earlier, looking in reasonable external condition for a locomotive that is about to be cut up. It was the first of the 'A3s', apart from *Humorist*, to receive the trough deflectors, in October 1960.
Gavin Morrison

2549/60050 *Persimmon*

Built new as 'A1'	October 1924; entered traffic as 'A3' 15 December 1943
Renumbered	518 (18 March 1946); 50 (8 July 1946); E50 (3 February 1948); 60050 (18 August 1948)
Liveries (as 'A3')	Black December 1943 LNER green April 1947 BR blue July 1949 BR green September 1952
Allocations (as 'A3')	Grantham 15 December 1943 King's Cross 27 October 1946 Grantham 30 May 1948 King's Cross 16 June 1948 Neasden 3 February 1949 King's Cross 3 July 1955 Neasden 9 October 1955 King's Cross 24 June 1956 Grantham 16 September 1956 New England 17 June 1962
Withdrawn	11 June 1963; to Doncaster Works for scrapping, 9 August 1963

Upper right:

Persimmon received the number 50 on 8 July 1946 after having run with the temporary number 518 during the LNER numbering reorganisation. All the 'A3s' were allocated numbers between 501 and 578, but they were actually applied to only 20 locomotives. *Persimmon* is shown making fine progress at the head of the down 'Yorkshire Pullman' at New Southgate on 11 October 1947. After nationalisation it received an 'E' prefix to the number 50, which it kept for six months before becoming No 60050. *E. R. Wethersett*

Centre right:

This fine study shows off the handsome appearance of the single-chimney 'A3'. *Persimmon* is just leaving Grantham on a down express to Newcastle in 1958, no doubt after the customary change of locomotives at this location. *L. Perrin*

Lower right:

The fireman is busy replenishing the tender with water as *Persimmon* pauses at platform 14 at York with a down express on 26 June 1960. The double chimney had been fitted in April 1959, but the deflectors were not attached until October 1961.
Gavin Morrison

2550/60051 *Blink Bonny*

Built new as 'A1'	October 1924; entered traffic as 'A3' 17 November 1945
Renumbered	51 (24 August 1946); 60051 (25 September 1948)
Liveries (as 'A3')	Black November 1945 LNER green May 1947 BR blue November 1950 BR green December 1952
Allocations (as 'A3')	Grantham 17 November 1945 King's Cross 27 October 1946 Neasden 3 February 1949 Grantham 15 November 1953 Copley Hill 2 May 1954 Heaton 15 September 1957, followed by eight transfers between Gateshead, Heaton and Darlington until 15 December 1963
Withdrawn	23 November 1964 (last in North Eastern Region); sold to Hughes Bolckow, North Blyth, for scrap, January 1965

Above:

One certainly cannot tell from this picture, but *Blink Bonny* was actually in the BR blue livery underneath all the dirt! This fine picture was taken at Harefield on the Great Central when the locomotive was heading the 12.15 from Marylebone on 12 May 1951. *E. R. Wethersett*

Below:

Blink Bonny spent 12 years as an 'A3' allocated to the Eastern Region before it was transferred to the North East. Its last allocation was at Leeds Copley Hill for just over three years, where it shared the top duties with the 'A1s'. Here it is seen on the down 'Queen of Scots' in April 1956 just south of Newark station. *D. Penney*

Above:
Blink Bonny was transferred from the Eastern to the North Eastern Region in September 1957, and this picture shows it on Neville Hill shed, Leeds, in a very dirty state when allocated to Gateshead. The date is 8 June 1961, by which time most of the main-line workings from the shed were going over to diesels. No 60051 had received its double chimney in August 1959, although the deflectors were not added till March 1962. *Gavin Morrison*

Right:
As *Blink Bonny* was the last 'A3' in the North Eastern Region, it enjoyed celebrity status for its last few months and was used on several rail tours. In immaculate condition, due to attention from Heaton shed, or possibly enthusiasts, it is seen on what was probably its only visit to Derby shed, on 18 April 1964, having worked the 'South Yorkshireman' rail tour. This had started out behind *Flying Scotsman* over the Woodhead route, and later in the day it visited Crewe via Uttoxeter. *Gavin Morrison*

Above:
Carlisle Upperby is the unusual location for this picture of *Prince Palatine* taken on 7 June 1965. It is looking extremely clean, but I believe this was because it had been on rail tour duties two days earlier. Its numberplate is in the lower position, and the trough deflectors fitted in October 1962 are shown to advantage. The yellow stripe on the cabside can just be seen, indicating that the locomotive was banned from working under the electric wires south of Crewe. *Gavin Morrison*

2551/60052 *Prince Palatine*

Built new as 'A1'	November 1924; entered traffic as 'A3' 8 August 1941
Renumbered	520 (5 April 1946); 52 (11 May 1946); 60052 (7 October 1948)
Liveries (as 'A3')	Black August 1941
	BR green June 1947
	BR blue May 1949
	BR green April 1952
Allocations (as 'A3')	Grantham 8 August 1941
	Copley Hill 28 September 1943
	New England 29 May 1944
	Doncaster 12 December 1948
	Leicester Central 22 May 1949
	Neasden 4 July 1954
	Leicester Central 5 December 1954
	Copley Hill 28 August 1955
	Heaton 15 September 1957
	Gateshead 5 January 1958
	Darlington 19 June 1960
	Gateshead 18 December 1960
	Heaton 9 September 1962
	Darlington 9 December 1962
	Heaton 2 June 1963
	Gateshead 16 June 1963
	St Margarets 25 August 1963
Withdrawn	17 January 1966 (last of the class); sold for scrap to P. W. McLellan, Langloan, 20 June 1966

Above:
Prince Palatine received its double chimney during a general overhaul at Doncaster in November 1958. While allocated to Gateshead it is shown at the north end of York station, about to leave with a down King's Cross-Newcastle express on 5 June 1960. It was allocated to 10 different sheds during its career. *Gavin Morrison*

Below:
As can be seen from the allocations list, *Prince Palatine* was reallocated 16 times as an 'A3', but even more unusual was that this included the Eastern, North Eastern and Scottish Regions. It had its last general repair at Doncaster in October 1962, then it visited Darlington Works for a casual light repair in May 1965. Its last visit to works was for a non-classified repair at Inverurie in August 1965. It spent more than six years on the Great Central, and this powerful picture shows it leaving Marylebone station at the head of the 'Master Cutler' in the 1950s. *F. R. Hebron*

2552/60053 *Sansovino*

Built new as 'A1'	November 1924; entered traffic as 'A3' 2 September 1943
Renumbered	521 (16 March 1946); 53 (30 November 1946); 60053 (5 February 1949)
Liveries (as 'A3')	Black September 1943 LNER green October 1947 BR blue June 1950 BR green May 1952
Allocations (as 'A3')	Copley Hill 2 September 1943 New England 26 December 1944 Leicester Central 7 February 1949 Doncaster 22 May 1949 Grantham 31 May 1949 Copley Hill 2 May 1954 Gateshead 15 September 1957 Darlington 7 December 1958 Gateshead 7 June 1959 Darlington 18 June 1961 Gateshead 17 December 1961 Heaton 9 September 1962 St Margarets 21 April 1963 (on loan) Heaton 16 May 1963
Withdrawn	27 May 1963; cut up at Doncaster Works

Above:
Sansovino was attached to a new-type non-corridor tender in September 1943, which ran with the locomotive until withdrawal. The signalbox at Chaloners Whin, just south of York, is clearly shown in this picture of *Sansovino* passing with an up express on 5 August 1951, which was during the five years that it was allocated to Grantham. *E. R. Wethersett*

Above:
Sansovino was named after the racehorse that won the Derby in 1924. The locomotive's double chimney was fitted in November 1958, and it was one of the 22 members of the class not to receive the trough smoke deflectors. In fine external condition, it is at Darlington shed on 11 October 1961 on main-line stand-by duties. *Gavin Morrison*

Above:
Prince of Wales in LNER apple green must have been a memorable sight in the snow near Potters Bar as it headed towards King's Cross on 22 February 1947. Originally the locomotive was named *Manna* up to December 1926, when it became *Prince of Wales*. It ran with a GNR-type tender with coal rails during its entire career. *E. R. Wethersett*

Below:
A fine night shot of *Prince of Wales* on York shed, with the double chimney and deflectors that it had received in May 1962 and June 1964 respectively. *C. P. Walker*

2553/60054 *Prince of Wales*

Built new as 'A1'	December 1924; entered traffic as 'A3' 28 July 1943
Renumbered	522 (17 March 1946); 54 (23 September 1946); 60054 (9 April 1948)
Liveries (as 'A3')	Black July 1943 LNER green October 1946 BR blue April 1950 BR green November 1951
Allocations (as 'A3')	New England 28 July 1943 Leicester Central 6 February 1949 King's Cross 10 June 1956 Grantham 16 June 1957 Doncaster 8 September 1963 New England 20 October 1963
Withdrawn	28 June 1964; sold to R. A. King, Norwich, for scrap, August 1964

2554/60055 *Woolwinder*

Built new as 'A1'	December 1924; entered traffic as 'A3' 3 June 1942
Renumbered	55 (28 September 1946); 60055 (4 June 1948)
Liveries (as 'A3')	Black June 1942 LNER green October 1946 BR blue April 1950 BR green November 1951
Allocations (as 'A3')	Gorton 3 June 1942 Grantham 22 November 1942 Copley Hill 2 October 1943 King's Cross 16 December 1944 Doncaster 4 June 1950 King's Cross 10 June 1956
Withdrawn	4 September 1961 while in Doncaster Works for repair

Right:
A fine, but undated, picture of *Woolwinder* about to enter Gasworks Tunnel while leaving King's Cross with a down express to Leeds Central and Bradford Exchange. The train would split at Wakefield Westgate. *Eric Treacy*

Above:
After a general repair in June 1958, *Woolwinder* returned to Top Shed (King's Cross) fitted with a double chimney, the first of the class to be so treated, except of course for No 60097 *Humorist* 21 years earlier in 1937. The locomotive was obviously appreciated by the shed and was put to work on King's Cross-Newcastle diagrams as well as Leeds turns; in fact it covered 4,000 miles in an 11-day period during February and March 1960. This superb portrait, taken on 1 October 1958, shows *Woolwinder* fitted with an 'A4' boiler. No 60055 was one of five of the class not to be fitted with a Smith Stone speed indicator. *Ian Allan Library*

Above:
Woolwinder makes a superb sight as it passes Grove Road, Retford, and starts the climb to Askham Tunnel with an up Leeds-King's Cross express in January 1959, the returning working of the previous Friday night's 'Yorkshire Pullman'; note the reversed headboard.
D. Penney

Right:
Woolwinder was one of the four members of the class to be fitted with the wing deflectors, but they were not a success. It is surprising that they were fitted at all, as *Humorist* had also been tried with them without success 20 years earlier. *Woolwinder* is seen leaving Peterborough with a down express during May 1960. *P. Ransome-Wallis*

2555/60056 *Centenary*

Built new as 'A1'	February 1925; entered traffic as 'A3' 16 August 1944
Renumbered	56 (10 July 1946); 60056 (18 May 1949)
Liveries (as 'A3')	Black August 1944 LNER green September 1947 BR blue May 1949 BR green May 1952
Allocations (as 'A3')	Doncaster 16 August 1944 Grantham 6 December 1944 King's Cross 27 October 1946 Copley Hill 30 May 1948 Doncaster 9 September 1951 Grantham 7 October 1951 Doncaster 25 May 1952 King's Cross 22 June 1952 Grantham 15 February 1953
Withdrawn	13 May 1963 while in Doncaster for repair, where it was cut up

Above:
Centenary, in splendid external condition during its eight-month spell at King's Cross in 1952, makes a superb sight as it heads a down express near New Southgate on 20 September of that year. *E. R. Wethersett*

Below:
In sharp contrast to the previous picture, *Centenary* is seen in the yard at Copley Hill shed on 16 March 1962. The double chimney was fitted in July 1959 and the deflectors in August 1961, when the locomotive received its last general repair. No 60056 was unusual, especially during the 1953 to 1963 period, in spending more than 10 consecutive years at Grantham. *Gavin Morrison*

2556/60057 *Ormonde*

Built new as 'A1'	February 1925; entered traffic as 'A3' 11 January 1947
Renumbered	57 (September 1946); 60057 (16 June 1948)
Liveries (as 'A3')	LNER green January 1947 BR blue July 1949 BR green October 1952
Allocations (as 'A3')	Haymarket 11 January 1947 Carlisle Canal 23 April 1961 Haymarket 15 May 1961 St Margarets 13 December 1961
Withdrawn	28 October 1963; sold to Arnott Young, Carmyle, for scrap, June 1964

Above:

With the help of a banker, *Ormonde* climbs the 1 in 41 Cowlairs Bank at the head of a morning Glasgow Queen Street-Edinburgh Waverley express, a duty it would have performed regularly during its long allocation to Haymarket shed. The date is 11 August 1949, which means it would be in BR blue livery. *E. R. Wethersett*

Below:

A powerful picture of an immaculate *Ormonde* heading towards the cutting before the tunnel on the climb from Inverkeithing to North Queensferry on 29 June 1954, on the up 12.40pm Aberdeen-Edinburgh Waverley train. The locomotive was converted to left-hand drive in October 1952. *E. D. Bruton*

Above:
Ormonde received its double chimney in September 1958, and is seen here arriving at Galashiels with the 12.53pm Edinburgh Waverley-Carlisle service on 1 April 1961. Back in May 1928 as an 'A1' *Ormonde* had a corridor tender for just one month. *D. J. Dippie*

Below:
On 7 April 1963, only six months before being withdrawn, *Ormonde* is on Doncaster shed awaiting its last visit to Doncaster Works for a casual repair. It also went to Cowlairs Works in July 1963 for a non-classified repair. It had received the deflectors in September 1961 during its last general overhaul. *Gavin Morrison*

Above:

In September 1957 *Blair Athol* moved from the Eastern to the North Eastern Region. On a day of diversions it is seen passing Lincoln at the head of a down King's Cross-Leeds Central express on 23 September 1956. The Copley Hill 56C shedplate can just be seen. The locomotive received the streamlined non-corridor tender in February 1955. *Eric Oldham*

Below:

Blair Athol presents a sorry sight three weeks after being withdrawn from Heaton shed, awaiting its last journey from Doncaster shed to the works for scrapping. The double chimney was fitted in October 1958, but it never received the smoke deflectors. Note that the position of the front numberplate has been raised from the previous picture. *Gavin Morrison*

2557/60058 Blair Athol	
Built new as 'A1'	February 1925; entered traffic as 'A3' 8 December 1945
Renumbered	58 (7 December 1946); 60058 (10 March 1949)
Liveries (as 'A3')	Black December 1945 LNER green April 1947 BR blue February 1951 BR green March 1953
Allocations (as 'A3')	Doncaster 8 December 1945 King's Cross 1 October 1950 Doncaster 29 October 1950 Copley Hill 13 June 1954 Gateshead 15 September 1957 Gateshead and Darlington, then Heaton 9 September 1962
Withdrawn	19 June 1963; to Doncaster Works, 10 July 1963, for cutting up

Right:
Tracery must have made a superb sight in the LNER apple green livery at the head of the down 'Queen of Scots' Pullman on 13 August 1948. Without a trace of exhaust, it is climbing towards the summit at Ardsley Tunnel, past Lofthouse. The colliery can just be seen in the background, where there was a serious mining disaster in the early 1960s. *E. R. Wethersett*

2558/60059 *Tracery*

Built new as 'A1'	March 1925; entered traffic as 'A3' 25 July 1942
Renumbered	59 (26 October 1946); 60059 (8 July 1948)
Liveries (as 'A3')	Black July 1942 LNER green April 1947 BR blue February 1951 BR green March 1953
Allocations (as 'A3')	Gorton 25 July 1942 King's Cross 29 December 1942 New England 16 April 1944 King's Cross 24 September 1944 Leicester Central 18 March 1951 King's Cross 7 April 1957
Withdrawn	17 December 1962 while at Doncaster for repair, where it was cut up

Centre right:
In immaculate Top Shed (King's Cross) external condition, *Tracery* is in the yard at Copley Hill shed on 7 August 1960 awaiting its next duty back to King's Cross; behind it is one of the local ex-Great Northern Class J6s. The double chimney was fitted during July 1958.
Gavin Morrison

Lower right:
Still in immaculate condition, but with the trough deflectors fitted in September 1961, *Tracery* rushes past the site of Tallington station, which closed to passengers on 15 June 1959, at the head of an afternoon King's Cross-Hull express. The locomotive was allocated to Gorton when new as an 'A3', but stayed for only a month. It spent around 10 years as an 'A1' and an 'A3' allocated to Great Central sheds, so it is surprising that it was one of five members of the class to exceed 2¼ million miles in service; in fact it covered 2,523,843 miles, the second highest for the class. *P. H. Wells*

2559/60060 *The Tetrarch*

Built new as 'A1'	April 1925; entered traffic as 'A3' 16 January 1942
Renumbered	528 (13 April 1946); 60 (22 June 1946); 60060 (1 October 1948)
Liveries (as 'A3')	Black January 1942 LNER green April 1947 BR blue January 1950 BR green August 1951
Allocations (as 'A3')	Gateshead 16 January 1942 Shared between Gateshead and Darlington until 23 September 1963
Withdrawn	23 September 1963; to Darlington Works for cutting up

Above:
A fine undated portrait of *The Tetrarch* after a general overhaul at Doncaster Works. As it is in BR green livery it must have been after August 1951 and before March 1959, when it received the double chimney. *Ian Allan Library*

Above:
The Tetrarch is at the head of an up fitted freight near Potters Bar on 14 May 1960. The double chimney was fitted during a general overhaul in March 1959, but the locomotive never received deflectors, even during its last general overhaul in August 1960. *K. L. Cook*

2560/60061 *Pretty Polly*

Built new as 'A1'	April 1925;
	entered traffic as 'A3' 6 May 1944
Renumbered	61 (18 November 1946);
	60061 (20 November 1948)
Liveries	Black May 1944
(as 'A3')	LNER green April 1947
	BR blue November 1950
	BR green August 1952
Allocations	New England 6 May 1944
(as 'A3')	Leicester Central 6 February 1949
	Doncaster 4 June 1950
	Copley Hill 26 November 1950
	King's Cross 18 February 1951
	Neasden 15 July 1951
	Grantham 22 February 1953
	King's Cross 29 August 1954
	Grantham 17 October 1954
	Doncaster 8 February 1959
	King's Cross 5 April 1959
	New England 13 September 1959
	King's Cross 8 November 1959
	Grantham 16 June 1963
Withdrawn	8 September 1963; cut up at Doncaster
	Works after 16 September 1963

Above right:
The locomotive was named *Pretty Polly* after the racehorse that won the Oaks, the 1,000 Guineas and the St Leger in 1904. It will be seen from the allocations that it moved sheds frequently and spent time at all the East Coast main line Eastern Region sheds, as well as two spells on the Great Central. Here it is running as No 61 in LNER green. The picture is undated, but the locomotive was at New England while numbered 61. It has just left Hadley Wood Tunnel at the head of a down King's Cross-Cleethorpes train. *R. F. Dearden*

Below:
Seen here on a Great Central up Manchester London Road-Marylebone express passing Willesden on 3 September 1949, *Pretty Polly* is still in LNER apple green livery, but numbered 60061, with 'British Railways' on the tender. This was during the locomotive's 16-month allocation to Leicester Central between February 1949 and June 1950. *E. R. Wethersett*

Left:
A fine portrait of *Pretty Polly* fitted with the wing deflectors that were attached to only four members of the class, as they did little good. No 60061 received its double chimney in October 1958.
P. Ransome-Wallis

Below:
Pretty Polly, fitted with trough deflectors in February 1962, is about to enter Stoke Tunnel at the head of a down express on 21 July of that year. *Gavin Morrison*

2561/60062 *Minoru*

Built new as 'A1'	May 1925; entered traffic as 'A3' 24 June 1944
Renumbered	62 (18 October 1946); E62 (4 March 1948); 60062 (6 July 1949)
Liveries (as 'A3')	Black June 1944 LNER green November 1947 BR blue July 1949 BR green October 1952
Allocations (as 'A3')	New England 24 June 1944 Gorton 7 July 1944 King's Cross 29 October 1944 Haymarket 11 April 1945 King's Cross 25 May 1945 Copley Hill 30 May 1948 Doncaster 9 September 1951 Grantham 15 February 1953 King's Cross 25 October 1953 New England 10 September 1961 Grantham 16 June 1963 Doncaster 8 September 1963 New England 20 October 1963
Withdrawn	26 December 1964; sold to R. A. King, Norwich, for scrap, February 1965

Above:
Minoru was unusual in being allocated to the ex-Great Central line, the Scottish Region (albeit only for six weeks) and the Eastern Region. It also ran with six different tenders. This picture shows it with a streamlined non-corridor type, at the head of an up Leeds Central to King's Cross express, passing Wortley Junction and crossing the ex-LNWR goods yard. The picture is undated, but it is after July 1949, when the locomotive received the number 60062 having previously been running as E62. It is carrying a 37B shedplate, indicating that it is allocated to Copley Hill. *Eric Treacy*

Below:
Minoru exchanged its streamlined non-corridor tender for a Great Northern-type with coal rails in February 1955. This fine picture shows it heading the up 'Flying Scotsman' at Markham Summit during September 1957, when it was allocated to Top Shed (34A). *D. Penney*

Above:
Now in immaculate condition with the double chimney fitted in February 1959, *Minoru* is seen at the head of an up express at Woolmer Green on 13 June 1959. *E. R. Wethersett*

Left:
Minoru is on Doncaster shed on 29 April 1962 in its final condition, the deflectors having been fitted in July 1961. Note the GNR-type tender with coal rails, which replaced the streamlined non-corridor one in February 1955. *Gavin Morrison*

Right:
On 23 April 1949 *Isinglass* is resplendent in LNER apple green livery, but with 'British Railways' on the tender, as it leaves Hadley Wood South Tunnel at the head of the 10.16am Harrogate-King's Cross express. *Isinglass* was one of the few 'A3s' to carry a temporary LNER number (531).
E. D. Bruton

2562/60063 *Isinglass*

Built new as 'A1'	July 1925; entered traffic as 'A3' 6 April 1946
Renumbered	531 (6 April 1946); 63 (3 July 1946); 60063 (21 January 1949)
Liveries (as 'A3')	Black April 1946 LNER green May 1947 BR blue March 1951 BR green November 1952
Allocations (as 'A3')	Doncaster 6 April 1946 King's Cross 4 June 1950 Grantham 9 September 1951 Neasden 22 February 1953 King's Cross 13 March 1955 Neasden 25 March 1956 King's Cross 24 June 1956 Grantham 16 September 1956 King's Cross 30 October 1960 Grantham 16 June 1963 Doncaster 8 September 1963 New England 20 October 1963
Withdrawn	28 June 1964; sold to R. A. King, Norwich, for scrapping, August 1964

Centre right:
A powerful picture of *Isinglass* working hard at the head of a down fitted freight passing Welwyn North on 10 September 1955. For a King's Cross 'A3' it appears rather dirty. During its entire career *Isinglass* was fitted with a GNR-type tender with coal rails.
S. Hulford

Lower right:
Isinglass is seen in Doncaster Works during its last visit when it received a casual light repair. The double chimney was fitted in February 1959 and the deflectors in August 1961. *Gavin Morrison*

2563/60064 Tagalie

Built new as 'A1'	August 1924; entered traffic as 'A3' 13 November 1942
Renumbered	64 (20 October 1946); E64 (30 January 1948); 60064 (9 July 1949)
Liveries (as 'A3')	Black November 1942 LNER green February 1947 BR blue July 1949 BR green February 1953
Allocations (as 'A3')	Haymarket 13 November 1942 Doncaster 2 July 1950 Grantham 9 July 1959
Withdrawn	4 September 1961 while at Doncaster Works, where it was cut up

Above:
Tagalie was the first of the batch of 'A1s' to be built by the North British Locomotive Company in July 1924, and was originally named *William Whitelaw* until July 1941, when that name was transferred to an 'A4'. While allocated to Doncaster, *Tagalie* emerges from Stoke Tunnel with a down express on 2 August 1958. *Gavin Morrison*

Below:
In terrible external condition, which was typical of Grantham locomotives at this time, *Tagalie* heads north on a down express past Beningborough on 6 August 1961, just one month before its withdrawal. It was one of the early withdrawals for the class and never received the trough deflectors, although a double chimney was fitted in June 1959. The locomotive was attached to a corridor tender for nearly five years in the early 1930s. Note the change of boiler type between the pictures — here it has a Type 107. *Gavin Morrison*

Right:

A superb picture of *Knight of Thistle* in LNER apple green livery, which it received in March 1947. It is at the head of the down 'Flying Scotsman' on 25 August of that year near Berwick. From new as an 'A1' in 1924 until July 1950 it was allocated to Scottish sheds.
E. R. Wethersett

2564/60065 *Knight of Thistle*

Built new as 'A1'	August 1924; entered traffic as 'A3' 23 March 1947 (the 'A1' prior to 1932 was named *Knight of the Thistle*)
Renumbered	65 (October 1946); 60065 (23 July 1948)
Liveries (as 'A3')	LNER green March 1947 BR blue November 1949 BR green December 1952
Allocations (as 'A3')	Haymarket 23 March 1947 King's Cross 2 July 1950 Grantham 9 September 1951 New England 17 June 1962 Grantham 16 June 1963 Doncaster 8 September 1963 New England 20 October 1963
Withdrawn	28 June 1964; sold to R. A. King, Norwich, for scrap, August 1964

Centre right:

Knight of Thistle spent nearly 11 years at Grantham between 1951 and 1962, and during this period it is seen working a diverted up express at Haxey on the Doncaster-Gainsborough line. *D. Penney*

Lower right:

This is *Knight of Thistle* in its final form on Copley Hill shed, Leeds, on 25 April 1962, and looking very clean for a Grantham engine. It was attached to a corridor tender for seven years between 1928 and 1935, but ran with this GNR type with coal rails from June 1937. The double chimney was fitted in October 1958 and the deflectors in November 1961. *Gavin Morrison*

2565/60066 *Merry Hampton*

Built new as 'A1'	August 1924; entered traffic as 'A3' 9 December 1945
Renumbered	66 (7 July 1946); 60066 (17 March 1948)
Liveries (as 'A3')	Black December 1945 LNER green December 1946 BR blue October 1949 BR green January 1953
Allocations (as 'A3')	Haymarket 9 December 1945 Doncaster 6 August 1950 King's Cross 1 October 1950 Doncaster 29 October 1950 King's Cross 10 June 1956 Doncaster 5 August 1956 King's Cross 16 June 1957 Doncaster 2 November 1958 King's Cross 4 May 1959 New England 13 September 1959 King's Cross 1 November 1959 Grantham 16 June 1963
Withdrawn	8 September 1963; to Doncaster Works for scrapping, 18 September 1963

Above:
After *Merry Hampton* left Scotland in 1950 it never moved away from sheds at the southern end of the East Coast main line. This powerful picture shows the locomotive in the BR blue livery at Gateshead with an Edinburgh Waverley-King's Cross express in 1950. *Eric Treacy*

Left:
Merry Hampton approaches Retford at Grove Road heading a down King's Cross-Leeds Central express in August 1957. *D. Penney*

Right:
Fresh out of 'The Plant' at Doncaster, *Merry Hampton* is on a running-in turn between Leeds Central and Doncaster after its last general overhaul. It received the deflectors in October 1961, and the date of the picture is 25 April 1962. *Gavin Morrison*

Above:
The high cab roof ventilator is clearly seen on *Merry Hampton* as it climbs towards Stoke Summit at the head of an up express on 17 June 1961, having just passed under the old 'A1' road bridge south of Grantham. It received its double chimney in October 1958. *Gavin Morrison*

Left:
On a hot summer's day in 1957, when it was allocated to Doncaster, *Ladas* heads a diverted down express past Haxey. *D. Penney*

2566/60067 *Ladas*

Built new as 'A1'	August 1924; entered traffic as 'A3' 4 November 1939
Renumbered	67 (13 October 1946); 60067 (30 July 1948)
Liveries (as 'A3')	LNER green November 1939 Black May 1942 LNER green April 1947 BR blue February 1950 BR green September 1951
Allocations (as 'A3')	Eastfield, Glasgow 4 November 1939 St Margarets 2 February 1940 Haymarket 26 November 1940 King's Cross 2 July 1950 Grantham 9 September 1951 Doncaster 18 May 1952 King's Cross 22 June 1952 Doncaster 18 October 1953 Grantham 14 June 1959 New England 13 September 1959 King's Cross 1 November 1959
Withdrawn	29 December 1962; to Doncaster Works for scrapping, January 1963

Centre left:
On 5 September 1959, in absolutely terrible condition, *Ladas* passes under the 'A1' road bridge south of Grantham and heads towards Stoke Tunnel with an up express; it was allocated to Grantham shed at the time. *Ladas* was the first 'A1' to be converted after a period of over 11 years in November 1939. It is attached to a new-type non-corridor tender, which it received in July 1930 and retained until withdrawal. It received the double chimney in April 1959. *Gavin Morrison*

Lower left:
Now in fine external condition, and allocated to Top Shed, King's Cross, *Ladas* climbs past Copley Hill heading the 12.30pm Leeds Central to King's Cross train on 12 October 1961. The deflectors were fitted in July 1961. *Gavin Morrison*

2567/60068 *Sir Visto*

Built new as 'A1'	September 1924; entered traffic as 'A3' 10 December 1948
Renumbered	68 (August 1946); 60068 (September 1948)
Liveries (as 'A3')	LNER green December 1948 BR blue October 1950 BR green August 1952
Allocation (as 'A3')	Carlisle Canal
Withdrawn	27 August 1962; to Doncaster Works for cutting up, 27 August 1962

Above:
Sir Visto was the last 'A1' to be converted to an 'A3', 24 years after entering service. On 10 January 1959 it is seen entering Carlisle station with the empty stock for the 2pm train to Newcastle. Later in the afternoon it headed north on the down 'Waverley' express. *R. Leslie*

Below:
Sir Visto was seldom seen away from its duties on the Waverley route, and is shown here departing from Longtown on the 2.36pm Edinburgh Waverley-Carlisle stopping train on 21 May 1960. The double chimney was fitted during a general repair in April 1959, but deflectors were not authorised for Carlisle Canal 'A3s' as they were in the London Midland Region. *R. Leslie*

Above:

Sceptre races south at 72mph towards York past Pilmoor at the head of an afternoon Newcastle-Birmingham New Street express. The train left Darlington at 4.48pm and was allowed 42 minutes start-to-stop for the 44 miles to York, which made it a favourite with the train time-keepers. The date is 10 August 1957 when the locomotive was allocated to Heaton, which was responsible for this working. *Gavin Morrison*

Below:

During its time as an 'A3' *Sceptre* was allocated to a variety of sheds, the most interesting being Holbeck, Leeds, for seven months. It was one of Holbeck's better 'A3s', and during its brief spell it worked the Scottish expresses over the Settle & Carlisle line. It received its double chimney in September 1959, and on 7 June 1961 is seen passing Holbeck Low Level station, which had closed on 7 July 1958, at the head of the down 'Thames-Clyde Express'. The Holbeck Locomotive Inspector, Albert Pullan, is leaning out of the cab, and the driver is a well-known character, Tommy Warren. The locomotive did not have deflectors fitted. *Gavin Morrison*

2568/60069 *Sceptre*	
Built new as 'A1'	September 1924; entered traffic as 'A3' 31 May 1942
Renumbered	537 (24 March 1946); 69 (26 May 1946); 60069 (8 July 1948)
Liveries (as 'A3')	Black May 1942 LNER green January 1947 BR blue January 1951 BR green July 1952
Allocations (as 'A3')	York 31 May 1942 Heaton 28 March 1943 Tweedmouth 14 September 1958 Copley Hill 12 June 1960 Holbeck 20 November 1960 Copley Hill 11 June 1961 Ardsley 10 September 1961
Withdrawn	1 October 1962; to Doncaster Works for scrapping, 27 May 1963

2569/60070 *Gladiateur*

Built new as 'A1'	September 1924; entered traffic as 'A3' 18 January 1947
Renumbered	538 (March 1946); 70 (June 1946); 60070 (27 August 1948)
Liveries (as 'A3')	LNER green January 1947 BR green February 1952
Allocations (as 'A3')	Gateshead and Darlington to 6 December 1959 Copley Hill 12 June 1960 Holbeck 20 November 1960 Copley Hill 11 June 1961 Ardsley 10 September 1961 Neville Hill 16 June 1963 Gateshead 8 December 1963
Withdrawn	4 May 1964; sold to A. Draper, Hull, for scrap, July 1964

Above right:
Gladiateur must have made a superb sight at the head of this down freight train near Berwick on 25 August 1947. It had received the apple green livery in January 1947 while at Doncaster for conversion to an 'A3', and as it spent a considerable amount of time allocated to Darlington on main-line stand-by duties it did not have a general repair between August 1948 and February 1952, and so became one of the two members of the class not to receive the blue livery. *E. R. Wethersett*

Below:
Gladiateur was allocated to three Leeds sheds, and is shown here at Farnley Junction; it is extremely unlikely that it ever visited the fourth Leeds shed at Stourton. 'A3s' were too big for the turntables inside Holbeck shed, so when washouts were due they were sent to Neville Hill or occasionally Farnley Junction, which I believe was the reason for this visit. *Gladiateur* went for a general overhaul one month after its time at Holbeck, which was surprising as there was very little work for the locomotive in late 1960. The double chimney was fitted in April 1959 and the deflectors in September 1961.
Gavin Morrison

Above:
Humble duties for *Tranquil* while allocated to Neville Hill shed, Leeds, in 1945. It is shown passing Cross Gates at Leeds heading east with a breakdown train. The locomotive is in LNER black livery, but does not appear to have been cleaned since a visit to Doncaster Plant in October 1944 when it became an 'A3'.
E. R. Wethersett

Left:
There are no details available for this fine picture, but the locomotive is obviously leaving York with a down express, and it must have been taken between May 1948 and July 1950 when *Tranquil* carried the distinctive BR purple livery. Only seven 'A3s' received this livery. *Eric Treacy*

Right:
Tranquil awaits its next duty on Copley Hill shed, Leeds, on 6 March 1962. The deflectors were fitted in November 1961.
Gavin Morrison

2570/60071 *Tranquil*

Built new as 'A1'	September 1924; entered traffic as 'A3' 28 October 1944
Renumbered	71 (27 October 1946); 60071 (18 May 1948)
Liveries (as 'A3')	Black October 1944 LNER green October 1947 BR purple May 1948 BR blue July 1950 BR green November 1951
Allocations (as 'A3')	York 28 October 1944 Neville Hill 29 September 1945 Gateshead and Darlington 6 May 1946 Heaton 9 September 1962 Gateshead 16 June 1963
Withdrawn	12 October 1964; sold to A. Draper, Hull, for scrap, December 1964

Right:
One month after the general overhaul when it received its double chimney, *Tranquil* is at the head of an up express climbing Gamston Bank in August 1958. *D. Penney*

Above:
Sunstar makes a particularly unspectacular departure from York on 14 June 1958 at the head of a 12-coach down express when it was a Heaton locomotive. It received the new-type non-corridor tender in October 1940 and kept it until withdrawal. *Gavin Morrison*

Below:
Sunstar had an eight-month spell allocated to Leeds Holbeck for working the Scottish expresses, and is seen here on the down 'Thames-Clyde Express' crossing the River Eden at Etterby Junction, Carlisle, on its way north. This was another locomotive to receive a general repair immediately after it left Holbeck. The double chimney was fitted in July 1959 and, surprisingly, deflectors were not fitted during its last general repair in November 1960. *Gavin Morrison*

2571/60072 *Sunstar*

Built new as 'A1'	September 1924; entered traffic as 'A3' 12 July 1941
Renumbered	72 (27 July 1946); E72 (5 March 1948); 60072 (19 August 1948)
Liveries (as 'A3')	Black July 1941
	LNER green March 1948
	BR blue August 1949
	BR green June 1952
Allocations (as 'A3')	Gateshead 12 July 1941
	Heaton 28 March 1943
	Tweedmouth 14 September 1958
	Copley Hill 12 June 1960
	Holbeck 20 November 1960
	Heaton 16 July 1961
Withdrawn	22 October 1962; cut up at Doncaster Works, 22 May 1963

2572/60073 *St Gatien*

Built new as 'A1'	October 1924;
	entered traffic as 'A3' 10 November 1945
Renumbered	73 (27 October 1946);
	60073 (31 March 1949)
Liveries (as 'A3')	Black November 1945
	LNER green April 1947
	BR blue December 1950
	BR green June 1952
Allocations	York 10 November 1945
(as 'A3')	Heaton 6 May 1946
	Gateshead 16 June 1963
Withdrawn	19 August 1963;
	cut up at Darlington Works, 31 August 1963

Above right:

St Gatien spent 36 years as an 'A1' and 'A3' allocated to either Gateshead or Heaton sheds, which must have made it one of Newcastle's longest-serving Pacifics. It briefly ran with a streamlined non-corridor tender for 10 months in 1937, which it then swapped for the GNR type. Running in BR blue livery, *St Gatien* is seen north of Aycliffe on 2 August 1951 working a parcels train. *E. R. Wethersett*

Below:

On 26 January 1963 I was making extremely slow progress towards Rise Hill Tunnel to photograph the up 'Waverley' with a Class 45 'Peak' when *St Gatien* burst out of the south portal and into Dent cutting, well on time much to my surprise; the line had been blocked by snow here for a week. I had no time to move for obvious reasons, so had to contend with the less than perfect location. The locomotive is externally in the worst condition I ever saw an 'A3'. The double chimney was fitted in August 1958 and the deflectors in July 1961. *Gavin Morrison*

Above:

A portrait taken between April and July 1928 when *Harvester* was attached to a corridor tender and is known to have worked five return non-stop trips on the 'Flying Scotsman'. In July 1928 it received a GNR-type tender, which it kept until withdrawal. *Ian Allan Library*

Below:

Harvester was the fourth 'A1' to be converted to an 'A3', and 20 years later, on 16 August 1948, it is seen passing Chaloners Whin, south of York, at the head of a King's Cross-Edinburgh Waverley express, with coaching stock in chocolate and cream livery. It must have been quite a sight, as *Harvester* had recently been repainted in the purple livery, which was applied to only seven members of the class. Note the impressive signal gantry. *E. R. Wethersett*

Right:
Most of the 'A3s' allocated to Holbeck in 1960 were in poor condition when they arrived for their short stay, but the Neville Hill ones on the other side of Leeds were said to be in better mechanical order, if not externally, and they were often borrowed by Holbeck to work the Scottish expresses over the Settle & Carlisle line. Complete with 'Thames-Clyde Express' headboard, *Harvester* passes Dent on the down express on 9 April 1961. *Gavin Morrison*

2573/60074 *Harvester*

Built new as 'A1'	October 1924; entered traffic as 'A3' 17 April 1928
Renumbered	542 (7 April 1946); 74 74 (30 June 1946); 60074 (19 May 1948)
Liveries (as 'A3')	LNER green April 1928 Black July 1942 LNER green August 1947 BR purple May 1948 BR blue November 1950 BR green November 1952
Allocations (as 'A3')	Gateshead 17 April 1928 Haymarket 18 April 1928 Gateshead 5 July 1928 Haymarket 12 April 1937 Gateshead 21 February 1938 Neville Hill 2 December 1939 York 28 February 1940 Heaton 28 March 1943 Gateshead 3 November 1945 Neville Hill 6 February 1949 York 27 November 1950 Neville Hill 17 December 1950
Withdrawn	8 April 1963; to Doncaster Works for scrapping, 29 May 1963

Above:
Harvester heads the up 'Queen of Scots' on Wiske Moor water troughs on 1 August 1951. This was a working for which the locomotive will probably be best remembered, as it was a regular performer during its final 13 years at Neville Hill shed. The external condition hardly does credit to the shed for such a prestigious working. *E. R. Wethersett*

2574/60075 *St Frusquin*

Built new as 'A1'	October 1924; entered traffic as 'A3' 26 June 1942
Renumbered	75 (27 October 1946); 60075 (28 May 1948)
Liveries (as 'A3')	Black June 1942 LNER green October 1947 BR purple May 1948 BR blue December 1950 BR green June 1952
Allocations (as 'A3')	Gateshead, later Gateshead and Darlington 26 June 1942 Heaton 9 December 1962 Darlington 2 June 1963 Gateshead 15 December 1963
Withdrawn	13 January 1964; to Darlington Works for cutting up, 4 February 1964

Above:
St Frusquin appears to be in the BR purple livery, so this picture will have been taken between May 1948 and December 1950. The locomotive is leaving Edinburgh Waverley with an up express — note that it does not carry a Gateshead shedplate, but has 'G'HEAD' on the buffer beam.
Ian Allan Library

Below:
In terrible external condition *St Frusquin* races through Thirsk on 16 August 1960 at the head of the 12.30pm Newcastle-Bristol express. *R. Leslie*

Left:

On 17 June 1961 *St Frusquin* is climbing towards Stoke Tunnel past the site of Great Ponton station, which had closed to passengers on 15 September 1958 but stayed open for goods traffic until 29 April 1963. The double chimney was fitted during a general overhaul in August 1959, but in spite of another three visits to Doncaster Works it never carried the trough deflectors. It always ran with the Great Northern-type tender. *Gavin Morrison*

2575/60076 *Galopin*

Built new as 'A1'	October 1924; entered traffic as 'A3' 27 June 1941
Renumbered	76 (September 1946); 60076 (September 1948)
Liveries (as 'A3')	LNER green June 1941 Black October 1942 LNER green January 1947 BR green March 1952
Allocation (as 'A3')	Gateshead 27 June 1941; shared between Gateshead and Darlington until withdrawal
Withdrawn	29 October 1962; to Doncaster Works for cutting up, 17 April 1963

Below:

On 5 March 1961 *Galopin* is on Darlington shed on main-line stand-by duties, which it performed regularly over the years. It was the last of the class to retain the LNER apple green livery, and together with No 60070 *Gladiateur* it never sported the BR blue livery. The double chimney was fitted in June 1959, but the locomotive never received deflectors. *Gavin Morrison*

Left:
During its 14 years allocated to Heaton shed as an 'A3', *The White Knight* is seen at Grantham in LNER apple green livery waiting to take over a down express on 8 July 1948. It ran with a Great Northern tender between July 1943 and November 1953, when it received a new-type non-corridor example. Note the lining-out on the back of the tender in this livery.
H. C. Casserley

2576/60077 *The White Knight*

Built new as 'A1'	October 1924; entered traffic as 'A3' 10 July 1943
Renumbered	545 (24 March 1946); 77 (30 June 1946); 60077 (17 November 1948)
Liveries (as 'A3')	Black July 1943 LNER green November 1946 BR blue September 1950 BR green March 1953
Allocations (as 'A3')	York 10 July 1943 Heaton 6 May 1946 Holbeck 21 February 1960 Copley Hill 11 June 1961 Ardsley 10 September 1961 St Margarets 16 June 1963
Withdrawn	13 July 1964; sold to Arnott Young, Carmyle, for scrapping, October 1964

Centre left:
The White Knight was only five months out of Doncaster Works after a general overhaul when it arrived at Leeds Holbeck on 21 February 1960, so it was in better condition than many of the others. Here it is seen at the head of the down 'Thames-Clyde Express' just north of Marley Junction near Keighley on 9 July 1961. The double chimney was fitted in April 1959 and the deflectors in July 1961.
Gavin Morrison

Lower left:
The White Knight ended its days at St Margarets shed, Edinburgh, and is seen here in unusual circumstances going to the rescue of a Class 45 'Peak' that had caught fire on the up 'Waverley' near Newcastleton on 13 June 1964. *The White Knight* had been removed from a freight train and was withdrawn four weeks later. *W. S. Sellar*

Right:
A superb portrait of *Night Hawk* in immaculate condition at Darlington shed on 24 April 1955 during its six-month allocation for stand-by duties.
Ian Allan Library

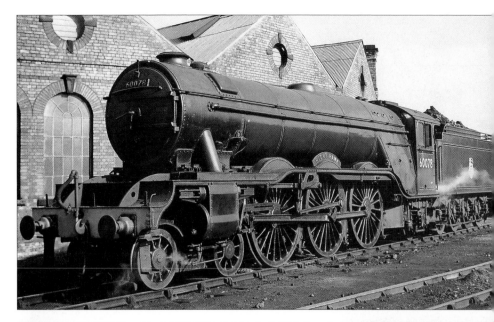

2577/60078 *Night Hawk*

Built new as 'A1'	October 1924; entered traffic as 'A3' 15 January 1944
Renumbered	78 (10 November 1946); 60078 (10 April 1948)
Liveries (as 'A3')	Black January 1944 LNER green February 1947 BR blue October 1950 BR green May 1952
Allocations (as 'A3')	York 15 January 1944 Neville Hill 29 September 1945 Gateshead 6 May 1946 Darlington 13 February 1955 Gateshead 7 August 1955 Heaton 9 June 1962
Withdrawn	22 October 1962; to Doncaster Works for cutting up, 9 May 1963

Centre right:
Night Hawk is ready to leave Newcastle with an up Edinburgh Waverley-King's Cross express on 16 July 1960. *R. Leslie*

Left:
Night Hawk's fire has been dropped for the last time as it languishes in Doncaster shed on 5 May 1963, awaiting its last journey to the Works for scrapping, which came four days later. The double chimney was fitted in February 1959 and the deflectors in March 1962. On the right is ex-Great Central 2-8-0 No 63618. *Gavin Morrison*

2578/60079 *Bayardo*

Built new as 'A1'	October 1924; entered traffic as 'A3' 22 May 1928
Renumbered	79 (7 November 1946); 60079 (18 March 1948)
Liveries (as 'A3')	LNER green May 1928
	Black January 1942
	LNER green March 1947
	BR blue May 1950
	BR green January 1952
Allocations (as 'A3')	Heaton 22 May 28
	Doncaster 23 August 1937
	Haymarket 11 September 1937
	Heaton 31 January 1938
	Gateshead 21 January 1940
	Heaton 6 January 1945
	Gateshead 28 May 1945
	Carlisle Canal 30 May 1948
Withdrawn	11 September 1961 while at Doncaster Works for repair

Upper left:
There is virtually no information regarding this early picture of *Bayardo* apparently at the head of the up 'Flying Scotsman'. *Bayardo* will be remembered by most enthusiasts as being a Carlisle Canal locomotive, but as can be seen from the allocations list, it moved around considerably before being allocated to 68E (later 12C). *Ian Allan Library*

Centre left:
Bayardo was the first 'A3' to have the 60000 added to its number of 79 on 18 March 1948. It is shown here with the lightweight 2pm Carlisle-Newcastle express at Dilston Crossing near Corbridge on 22 June 1957. *R. Leslie*

Right:
Bayardo received its double chimney during its last visit to Doncaster for a general overhaul in January 1960, but by then, being allocated to the London Midland Region, it did not receive deflectors. It is seen here on the down 'Waverley' on 11 March 1961 about to leave Carlisle, where it had probably taken over from a Holbeck-allocated 'A3'. *R. Leslie*

2579/60080 *Dick Turpin*

Built new as 'A1'	November 1924; entered traffic as 'A3' 26 November 1942
Renumbered	80 (2 November 1946); 60080 (18 March 1949)
Liveries (as 'A3')	Black November 1942 LNER green August 1947 BR blue October 1950 BR green February 1952
Allocations (as 'A3')	Heaton 26 November 1942 Gateshead 31 August 1944 Heaton 3 November 1945 Holbeck 8 May 1960 Ardsley 11 June 1961 Neville Hill 16 June 1963 Gateshead 8 December 1963
Withdrawn	12 October 1964; sold to A. Draper, Hull, for scrapping, December 1964

Above right:
Dick Turpin was a Newcastle-allocated locomotive for the first 36 years of its career. Here we see it in the fine LNER apple green livery and numbered 80 at the head of a down King's Cross-Newcastle express on 10 July 1948 passing Chaloners Whin, south of York. *E. R. Wethersett*

Below:
Dick Turpin arrived at Leeds Holbeck in May 1960 to work the Scottish expresses over the Settle & Carlisle line, and stayed on these duties for just over a year. It is seen here passing Wortley Junction, Leeds, heading the down 'Waverley' on 16 May 1961. Once again, like some of the other Holbeck 'A3s', it went for a general overhaul four months after it was transferred to Ardsley, where there was relatively little work for it. The double chimney was fitted in October 1959 and the deflectors in November 1961. *Gavin Morrison*

2580/60081 *Shotover*

Built new as 'A1'	November 1924; entered traffic as 'A3' 16 February 1928
Renumbered	81 (1 December 1946); 60081 (3 June 1948)
Liveries (as 'A3')	LNER green February 1928 Black September 1943 LNER green October 1946 BR blue October 1949 BR green February 1953
Allocations (as 'A3')	Heaton 16 February 1928 Gateshead 29 September 1928 Heaton 5 March 1930 Neville Hill 2 December 1939 York 28 February 1940 Heaton 28 March 1943 Gateshead 3 November 1945 Neville Hill 6 February 1949
Withdrawn	1 October 1962; to Doncaster Works for scrapping, 28 May 1963

Upper left:
Shotover was the third 'A1' to be converted to an 'A3', and was sent to the Scottish Region for testing. As can be seen from the list of allocations, the locomotive remained within the North Eastern area for its entire career, and will be remembered for its final 13 years at Neville Hill, where it performed regularly on the 'Queen of Scots' and 'North Briton'. Here it is fitted with a corridor tender, which it carried between April 1928 and February 1929. The location is the turntable outside King's Cross station. *Ian Allan Library*

Centre left:
A powerful picture of *Shotover* running in the wartime black livery with only 'NE' on the tender. The date is 15 July 1946, the location Peascliffe, and the train a down King's Cross-Edinburgh express. A month later *Shotover* went to 'The Plant' and emerged in October in LNER apple green. *E. R. Wethersett*

Lower left:
On a damp morning *Shotover* waits at Leeds City Wellington Street to take over the 10.35am to Glasgow St Enoch, another occasion when Holbeck had borrowed a Neville Hill 'A3'. The fact that the photographer was about to enjoy a footplate trip to Carlisle may have influenced the choice of locomotive. It received its double chimney in October 1958 but it never carried deflectors. *Eric Treacy*

2581/60082 *Neil Gow*

Built new as 'A1'	November 1924; entered traffic as 'A3' 15 January 1943
Renumbered	82 (20 June 1946); 60082 (26 May 1948)
Liveries (as 'A3')	Black January 1943 LNER green May 1948 BR blue September 1949 BR green March 1952
Allocations (as 'A3')	Heaton 15 January 1943 Gateshead 13 June 1948 Darlington 14 September 1952 Gateshead 22 March 1953 Heaton 6 May 1956 Holbeck 8 May 1960 Heaton 16 July 1961 Gateshead 25 March 1962 Heaton 9 September 1962 Gateshead 16 June 1963
Withdrawn	2 September 1963; to Darlington Works for cutting up, 22 February 1964

Above right:
This atmospheric picture shows *Neil Gow* on 22 December 1956 at the north end of what was then platform 9 at York. The train is the 9.10am King's Cross-Newcastle Tyne Commission Quay, but there was dense fog all day, which was no doubt the reason why the train was 168 minutes late! One hopes the passengers caught their boat across the North Sea.
H. D. Ramsey

Below:
With the 'Thames-Clyde Express' headboard in place, *Neil Gow* is being prepared on Holbeck shed, Leeds, for the down working on 6 March 1961. *Gavin Morrison*

Above:
In fine external condition *Neil Gow* takes it slowly round the sharp curve at Bingley Junction, Shipley, as it heads the down 'Thames-Clyde Express' on 10 May 1961. The locomotive happens to be my favourite 'A3', only because I enjoyed several marvellous trips on its footplate over the Settle & Carlisle line when it was at Leeds Holbeck. The double chimney had been fitted in September 1959. *Gavin Morrison*

Left:
Neil Gow received its last general repair at Doncaster between 19 July and 25 August 1961, once again another case of an 'A3' having a general repair after it was transferred away from Leeds Holbeck. As can be seen, it left the Works with a Holbeck shedplate, although by the date of the picture, 31 August 1961, it was allocated to Heaton. The deflectors were fitted during this Works visit, and it was given a Type 107 boiler, which was previously fitted to 'A4' 60022 *Mallard*. *Gavin Morrison*

2582/60083 Sir Hugo

Built new as 'A1'	December 1924; entered traffic as 'A3' 17 December 1941
Renumbered	83 (20 October 1946); 60083 (27 May 1949)
Liveries (as 'A3')	Black December 1941 LNER green August 1946 BR blue May 1949 BR green September 1952
Allocations (as 'A3')	Heaton 17 December 1941 Gateshead 16 June 1963
Withdrawn	18 May 1964; sold to Hughes Bolckow, North Blyth, for scrapping, August 1964

Right:
Sir Hugo was the last of the North British-built 'A1s' and was remarkable for spending its entire career as an 'A1' and 'A3' allocated to the Newcastle sheds; it was even sent for scrapping in the North East. Unfortunately there are no details of this fine picture of it heading north somewhere in the Alnmouth area, with the North Sea on the left, some time before it received its double chimney in September 1959. *Ian Allan Library*

Below:
After the closure of Carlisle Canal shed on June 1963, steam locomotives working over the Waverley route from Edinburgh were serviced at Carlisle Kingmoor, where *Sir Hugo* is seen on 6 April 1963. Its last general repair was in February 1962 when it received the trough deflectors. *Gavin Morrison*

Left:
Trigo was one of seven 'A3s' to receive the BR purple livery. 'G'HEAD' can just be made out on the buffer beam, which means that the picture was taken between May 1948, when it became purple, and September 1949, when it started its 14 years allocated to Neville Hill. It is taking water at an unidentified location.
Ian Allan Library

2595/60084 *Trigo*

Built as 'A3'	
Entered traffic	22 February 1930
Renumbered	84 (27 October 1946); 60084 (31 May 1948)
Liveries	LNER green when new
	Black October 1942
	LNER green February 1947
	BR purple May 1948
	BR blue June 1949
	BR green August 1952
Allocations	New to Gateshead
	Heaton 28 March 1943
	Gateshead 3 November 1945
	Neville Hill 4 September 1949
	Gateshead 8 December 1963
Withdrawn	23 November 1964; sold to Hughes Bolckow, North Blyth, for scrap, January 1965

Left:
Trigo received its double chimney in July 1958, and is shown in clean condition on Leeds Holbeck shed being prepared for a trip north over the Settle & Carlisle line. Note that the Neville Hill shedplate is now 55H. *Gavin Morrison*

Right:
Deflectors were fitted to *Trigo* in January 1962, and it will be seen that the front numberplate has been lowered since the previous picture. At the head of the down 10.35am Leeds-Glasgow St Enoch train on 20 June 1962, *Trigo* slows for the sharp Shipley Curve, at Leeds Junction, and passes a Midland '4F' on a pick-up freight.
Gavin Morrison

Right:
Taken during its 19 continuous years allocated to Heaton shed, *Manna* is passing Markham Moor during 1958 at the head of a down express. It is running with a new-type non-corridor tender, which it exchanged for a GNR type with coal rails in April 1962, as shown in the next picture. *D. Penney*

Centre right:
Manna has just left the Works two days earlier after its last general overhaul on 29 April 1962, when the deflectors were fitted. It has also been attached to a Great Northern-type tender for the first time in its career. *Gavin Morrison*

Below right:
Manna does not appear to have been cleaned since it left the Works just under two years ago, judging by this picture taken at Newcastle Central on 10 February 1964, when it was about to leave with the 4.30pm service to Berwick. *B. J. Ashworth*

2596/60085 *Manna*

Built as 'A3'	
Entered traffic	22 February 1930
Renumbered	85 (27 October 1946); 60085 (3 July 1948)
Liveries	LNER green when new Black April 1943 LNER green December 1947 BR blue November 1949 BR green December 1952
Allocations	New to Gateshead Heaton 28 March 1943 Gateshead 14 February 1944 Heaton 31 August 1944 Gateshead 16 June 1963
Withdrawn	12 October 1964; sold to A. Draper, Hull, for scrap, December 1964

2597/60086 *Gainsborough*

Built as 'A3'

Entered traffic 7 April 1930

Renumbered 86 (27 October 1946);
60086 (16 September 1948)

Liveries LNER green when new
Black June 1942
LNER green May 1947
BR blue May 1949
BR green June 1952

Allocations New to Gateshead
Doncaster 15 March 1936
Gateshead 17 July 1936
Heaton 30 September 1939
Neville Hill 2 December 1939
York 29 February 1940
Heaton 28 March 1943
Gateshead 30 November 1944
Neville Hill 6 February 1949

Withdrawn 18 November 1963;
to Darlington Works for
scrapping, 31 December 1963

Above:
Gainsborough is in fine external condition in Doncaster Works yard, where it is awaiting a general overhaul on 3 April 1959. The double chimney was fitted during this visit. *Gavin Morrison*

Below:
Gainsborough has just arrived at Leeds City at the head of the 9.55am Newcastle-Liverpool train, and is being uncoupled in order to hand over to an LMS 'Rebuilt Scot' and 'Patriot', which will take the train over the Pennines to Liverpool. *Gainsborough* was never fitted with the trough deflectors, and was another 'A3' to have 14 continuous years allocated to Neville Hill shed. *Gavin Morrison*

2598/60087 *Blenheim*

Built as 'A3'
Entered traffic June 1930
Renumbered 565 (21 March 1946);
87 (27 October 1946);
60087 (20 October 1948)
Liveries LNER green when new
Black June 1944
LNER green June 1947
BR blue August 1950
BR green July 1952
Allocations New to Gateshead
Doncaster 20 July 1937
Gateshead 13 October 1937
Haymarket 16 October 1937
Gateshead 8 February 1938
Haymarket 9 March 1939
Aberdeen 2 July 1940
Haymarket 18 October 1941
St Margarets 13 July 1960
Haymarket 28 November 1960
St Margarets 13 December 1961
Withdrawn 28 October 1963;
sold to Arnott Young, Carmyle,
for scrap, June 1964

Above right:
Blenheim moved around frequently during its early years and was allocated to three different regions until it settled down at Haymarket for 19 years from 1941. Obviously cleaners were at a premium there in 1952, judging by the external condition of No 60087 on 25 July 1952 as it heads the up 'Queen of Scots' near the border just north of Berwick. As it was ex-works from Doncaster after a general repair on 4 July, it had got very dirty by the 25th. *E. R. Wethersett*

Above:
Together with many well-known Haymarket Pacifics, *Blenheim* was stored minus its works and nameplates at Bathgate before being sold for scrap. Here it presents a sorry sight on 31 March 1964 awaiting its last call to Arnott Young for cutting up. The double chimney was fitted in August 1958 and the deflectors in February 1962. *Gavin Morrison*

2599/60088 *Book Law*

Built as 'A3'
Entered traffic 12 July 1930
Renumbered 88 (2 August 1946);
60088 (15 July 1948)
Liveries LNER green when new
Black March 1943
LNER green June 1947
BR blue March 1951
BR green February 1953
Allocations New to Gateshead
Haymarket 8 October 1937
Gateshead 23 January 1938
Heaton 28 March 1943
Gateshead 3 May 1943
Heaton 3 November 1945
Holbeck 8 May 1960
Heaton 16 July 1961
Gateshead 16 June 1963
Withdrawn 14 October 1963;
to Darlington Works for
scrapping, 15 November
1963

Above:
Looking immaculate in the LNER apple green livery, *Book Law* makes an impressive sight near Prestonpans at the head of an up freight on 23 April 1948. The Great Northern tender remained with the locomotive from March 1943.
E. R. Wethersett

Below:
Book Law spent 14½ years allocated to Heaton from November 1945 to May 1960. During this period, in 1958, before the double chimney was fitted in July 1959, it is seen leaving Retford with an up express. *D. Penney*

During its 14-month period at Leeds Holbeck, *Book Law* has been borrowed, probably by Neville Hill, to work the 10am Liverpool-Newcastle service. It is seen leaving Leeds City with the double chimney that was fitted in July 1959. *Gavin Morrison*

After *Book Law's* general overhaul in June 1961, it had five weeks at Holbeck before returning to its old area at Newcastle. During this overhaul, which was its last, it received the trough deflectors. It is seen here passing Wortley Junction, Leeds, on the down 'Waverley' on 28 June 1961. *Gavin Morrison*

Above:

An early picture of *Felstead* leaving York on the up 'Scarborough Flier'. The locomotive was originally attached to a corridor tender, but this was exchanged in February 1929 for the Great Northern type as shown. As can be seen from the allocations list, *Felstead* was unusual in being allocated to the Eastern, North Eastern and Scottish Regions. *E. R. Wethersett*

Below:

This was probably *Felstead's* only visit to Leeds Holbeck shed, where it arrived on 29 August 1963 after working the up 'Waverley' due to a failed Class 45 'Peak'; local 'Jubilee' No 45562 *Alberta* stands beyond. The double chimney was fitted in October 1959 and the trough deflectors in November 1961. Together with No 60090, No 60089 was the only 'A3' to be allocated to Dundee, if only for one month, and was unusual in being scrapped at Inverurie Works. *Gavin Morrison*

2743/60089 *Felstead*

Built as 'A3'
Entered traffic 22 August 1928
Renumbered 89 (18 September 1946); 60089 (3 September 1948)
Liveries LNER green when new
Black May 1942
LNER green September 1946
BR blue October 1950
BR green March 1952
Allocations New to Doncaster
Gateshead 15 March 1936
Doncaster 17 July 1936
Grantham 9 February 1941
King's Cross 19 May 1945
Haymarket 18 February 1951
Dundee 21 November 1960
St Margarets
  19 December 1960
Withdrawn 14 October 1963;
to Inverurie for scrapping,
2 November 1963,
completed by 21 February
1964

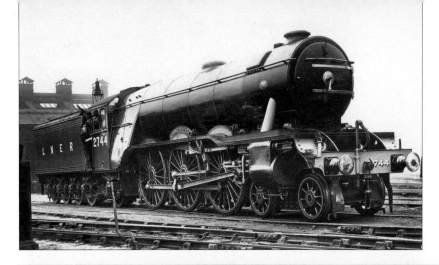

Right:
Due to the very serious accident at Castlecary on 10 December 1937, the original *Grand Parade* was a virtual write-off, and there was probably very little of the original in the rebuilt replacement, so there were really two *Grand Parades*. In this early picture, which was taken before December 1936, because it is fitted with a corridor tender, the original locomotive is seen at Top Shed, King's Cross. If one examines the allocations list, it will be seen that the locomotive was allocated to nine different sheds. *Ian Allan Library*

2744/60090 *Grand Parade*

Built as 'A3'	
Entered traffic	23 August 1928
Renumbered	90 (9 December 1946); 60090 (16 February 1949)
Liveries	LNER green when new Black November 1942 LNER green May 1947 BR blue November 1950 BR green May 1952
Allocations	New to King's Cross Haymarket 7 July 1937 Doncaster 31 March 1938 Grantham 1 July 1943 New England 11 April 1944 Leicester Central 16 February 1949 Grantham 16 May 1949 Doncaster 2 April 1950 Haymarket 2 July 1950 Dundee 21 November 1960 St Rollox 18 June 1962 Eastfield 31 December 1962 St Rollox 14 January 1963
Withdrawn	28 October 1963; to Cowlairs Works for scrapping, 24 January 1964

Centre right:
Grand Parade is seen ready to leave Edinburgh Waverley on the up 'Queen of Scots', which it will work as far as Newcastle Central. The photograph was probably taken in the early 1950s. *Ian Allan Library*

Lower right:
This portrait of *Grand Parade* was taken at Haymarket on 21 May 1961, with the double chimney that was fitted in August 1958. Deflectors were attached during a casual light repair in January 1963. *J. C. Haydon*

2745/60091 *Captain Cuttle*

Built as 'A3'	
Entered traffic	8 September 1928
Renumbered	91 (10 October 1946); 60091 (2 April 1948)
Liveries	LNER green when new
	Black February 1942
	LNER green October 1946
	BR purple April 1948
	BR blue November 1949
	BR green January 1953
Allocations	New to Doncaster
	Haymarket 24 October 1928
	Carlisle 26 October 1928
	Gateshead 30 May 1948; shared between Gateshead, Heaton and Darlington until withdrawal
Withdrawn	12 October 1964; sold for scrap to A. Draper, Hull, December 1964

Upper left:
Captain Cuttle was the first of the seven 'A3s' to receive the purple livery; it left 'The Plant' on 2 April 1948 with yellow lining, but was back in the paint shop by the 14th to receive cream and red lining. Here it is seen on 13 August 1949 climbing to Grantshouse with a down express, in the purple livery and showing the 'British Railways' lettering on the tender.
E. R. Wethersett

Centre left:
Captain Cuttle is leaving Grantham on 16 March 1957 having just taken over the down 'Northumbrian', which it will work through to Newcastle. *Gavin Morrison*

Right:
During one of its periods at Darlington shed for main-line stand-by duties, *Captain Cuttle* is shown on shed in its final form on 12 March 1962. The double chimney was fitted in March 1959 and the deflectors in October 1961. Note that the front numberplate is in the lower position.
Gavin Morrison

Above:
This early picture of *Fairway* was taken when it was allocated to King's Cross and running with a corridor tender. It is heading an up Newcastle express passing Greenwood on 14 September 1934. *E. R. Wethersett*

Below right:
Fairway is seen here in the yard at King's Cross on 12 February 1948 in the apple green livery. *C. C. B. Herbert*

2746/60092 *Fairway*

Built as 'A3',	
Entered traffic	November 1928
Renumbered	92 (October 1946);
	60092 (April 1949)
Liveries	LNER green when new
	Black July 1942
	LNER green June 1947
	BR blue November 1950
	BR green August 1952
Allocations	New to King's Cross
	Gateshead 10 November 1936
	King's Cross 15 December 1936
	Gateshead 14 January 1937
	Heaton 28 March 1943
	Holbeck 8 May 1960
	Ardsley 11 June 1961
	Gateshead 16 June 1963
Withdrawal	12 October 1964;
	sold for scrap to A. Draper,
	Hull, December 1964

Above:
Four weeks after its transfer to Leeds Holbeck, *Fairway* is passing Gretna Green on the up 'Thames-Clyde Express' on 4 June 1960, with the double chimney that it had acquired in November 1959.
Gavin Morrison

Left:
On 29 February 1964, a dismal foggy day when there were several 'Footex' specials from Newcastle to Manchester, all worked by 'A3s' to York or Leeds, *Fairway* is on York shed after working one of them. Its last visit to the Works for a non-classified repair had been in November 1961, when it received the trough deflectors.
Gavin Morrison

2747/60093 Coronach

Built as 'A3'	
Renumbered	93 (7 July 1946); 60093 (19 September 1948)
Entered traffic	24 November 1928
Liveries	LNER green when new Black February 1942 LNER green August 1947 BR blue October 1949 BR green May 1952
Allocations	New to Doncaster King's Cross 17 March 1930 Doncaster 3 May 1930 Haymarket 16 March 1939 Carlisle 23 January 1941
Withdrawn	24 April 1962; cut up in Doncaster Works

Above:
In 1931 *Coronach* was used for experiments in smoke deflection: the upper part of the smokebox was partitioned off to give an air duct to lift the smoke, but it was not successful. The picture shows the locomotive with this modification on the turntable just outside King's Cross station. *Ian Allan Library*

Below:
Coronach heads north past Parkhouse Halt, opened around 1937 to serve the adjacent RAF maintenance unit near Carlisle, at the head of the 1.28pm Carlisle-Edinburgh express on 19 April 1958. *R. Leslie*

Above:
Coronach received a double chimney in December 1958, but it never had deflectors. It was photographed at the head of the down 'Waverley' passing Kingmoor, north of Carlisle, just before crossing the West Coast main line on 4 April 1959. *R. Leslie*

Below:
Coronach spent its last 21 years allocated to Carlisle Canal shed, where it worked to Edinburgh over the Waverley route, although in this picture it is on Doncaster shed on 14 January 1962 after its last visit to the Works for a casual light repair. *Gavin Morrison*

Above:
Colorado spent only four months away from Scottish sheds, and here we see it crossing the Forth Bridge, together with Inspector Bell who was supervising the visit. The locomotive ran with a GNR-type tender until as late as December 1962, when it was attached to a new-type non-corridor example while having a casual light repair.
E. R. Wethersett

2748/60094 *Colorado*

Built as 'A3'	
Entered traffic	20 December 1928
Renumbered	94 (1 December 1946); 60094 (20 December 1948)
Liveries	LNER green when new Black May 1943 LNER green September 1947 BR blue May 1950 BR green April 1952
Allocations	New to Doncaster King's Cross 13 February 1929 Carlisle 5 April 1929 Haymarket 29 December 1947 St Margarets 13 December 1961 St Rollox 18 June 1962 Eastfield 31 December 1962 St Rollox 14 January 1963
Withdrawn	24 February 1964; to Henderson's of Airdrie for scrap, June 1964

2749/60095 Flamingo

Built as 'A3'	
Entered traffic	26 January 1929
Renumbered	558 (13 March 1946);
	95 (5 May 1946);
	60095 (19 September 1948)
Liveries	LNER green when new
	Black December 1942
	LNER green August 1947
	BR blue December 1950
	BR green May 1952
Allocations	New to Doncaster
	Carlisle 6 February 1929
Withdrawn	10 April 1961;
	cut up at Doncaster Works

Above:
This very early picture must have been taken in 1929 since *Flamingo* is attached to a GNR-type tender. It ran with a corridor tender for a month while still at Doncaster, then went back to the GNR type before finally receiving a streamlined non-corridor tender in February 1954. The picture appears to have been taken on Doncaster shed. *Ian Allan Library*

Centre left:
This very fine picture shows *Flamingo* on a lightweight duty passing Portobello with an express for Carlisle. The 68E shedplate and allocation name on the buffer beam stand out clearly. The locomotive's 32 years allocated to Carlisle Canal resulted in it achieving the lowest mileage for the class, at only 1,513,176 miles. *Flying Fox*, for example, achieved around 1.1 million more miles in only about six more years' service, but 1.5 million miles adds up to a lot of trips over the Waverley route. *Eric Treacy*

Lower left:
Flamingo is at the head of the down 'Waverley' on 18 May 1959, heading north near Scotch Dyke, north of Longtown. It received its double chimney in February 1959 but never carried deflectors. *R. Leslie*

Above:
Papyrus is probably the second most famous 'A3' after *Flying Scotsman*. This is due to its celebrated test runs in March 1935 between King's Cross and Newcastle, where it averaged 68.7mph for the 536.6-mile round trip and attained what was then a world record for steam of 108mph descending Stoke Bank. Here we see a very early picture of No 2750 in the yard at King's Cross, about to be turned and displaying the 'Flying Scotsman' headboard. *Ian Allan Library*

Below:
Not in the external condition normally associated with Haymarket Pacifics, *Papyrus* is shown on the Tay Bridge working the 11.50am up express from Dundee to Edinburgh Waverley on 23 July 1952. *E. R. Wethersett*

2750/60096 *Papyrus*

Built as 'A3'	
Renumbered	96 (11 November 1946); 60096 (27 October 1948)
Entered traffic	23 February 1929
Liveries	LNER green when new
	Black May 1943
	LNER green December 1947
	BR blue August 1949
	BR green April 1952
Allocations	New to King's Cross
	Haymarket 14 August 1937
	King's Cross 8 September 1937
	Doncaster 12 October 1937
	Grantham 11 March 1939
	King's Cross 27 October 946
	Haymarket 2 July 1950
	St Margarets 13 December 1961
Withdrawn	9 September 1963; sold to Arnott Young, Carmyle, for scrap, June 1964

Above:

Papyrus was remarkable not only for its 108mph but also because it had no fewer than eight tender changes during its career, being attached to every type except the streamlined non-corridor. November 1953 saw the last tender change to a Great Northern type, which it has in this picture on the Forth Bridge, hauling what looks like an up fish train on 31 July 1958. The double chimney was fitted that month. *E. R. Wethersett*

Left:

Papyrus was a very rare visitor to Leeds Holbeck on 9 April 1962 when allocated to St Margarets, having probably worked a sleeper from the north during the night. St Margarets shed did not give the locomotive the external attention it enjoyed at Haymarket during the previous 11 years it spent there. The deflectors were added in September 1961 when it received its last general overhaul. *Gavin Morrison*

2751/60097 *Humorist*

Built as 'A3'	
Entered traffic	7 March 1939
Renumbered	97 (27 May 1946);
	60097 (24 June 1948)
Liveries	LNER green when new
	Black August 1942
	LNER green September 1946
	BR blue November 1949
	BR green January 1956
Allocations	New to Doncaster
	Grantham 7 August 1942
	King's Cross
	27 October 1946
	Haymarket 2 July 1950
	Carlisle Canal
	6 January 1954
	Haymarket 21 February 1954
	St Margarets
	13 December 1961
Withdrawn	24 August 1963;
	to Doncaster Works for
	repair but withdrawn and cut
	up on 23 July 1963

Upper right:
Apart from *Flying Scotsman*, *Humorist* must have been the most frequently photographed 'A3', as its appearance was always being altered. Here we see the locomotive as originally built, at what appears to be Doncaster shed during the 1930s. It was attached to a Great Northern-type tender for its entire career.
Ian Allan Library

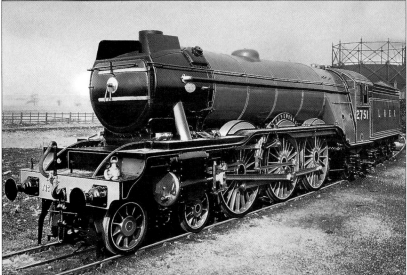

Centre right:
An official photograph of *Humorist* in early 1933 with the top of the smokebox cut away and wind vanes fitted. The authorities said that this had solved the drifting smoke problem, but no other members were thus converted, and at its next overhaul in January 1934 *Humorist* was returned to normal. *Ian Allan Library*

Lower right:
Humorist appears to be in ex-works condition, so it is possible that this picture was taken in July 1937 when it was fitted with a double blastpipe and chimney. It is at the head of a local Doncaster-Peterborough train at Barkston.
T. G. Hepburn

Left:
Humorist received the plain-pattern double chimney and further wind vanes in January 1938, and apparently the modification produced acceptable results as it ran in this condition until April 1947. It is seen here as No 97 in wartime black livery at Grantham. *T. G. Hepburn*

Centre left:
Nearly in its final condition, with smoke deflectors but without a rimmed chimney, *Humorist* is seen at Top Shed, King's Cross, in LNER apple green livery on 6 February 1948. *C. C. B. Herbert*

Lower left:
Apart from a later split smokebox handrail and lowered front numberplate, this picture from May 1958 shows *Humorist* in its final condition, passing Haymarket, its home shed for many years, on an Edinburgh Waverley-Aberdeen express; Edinburgh's famous castle can just be seen in the background. In spite of the improvements the double chimney brought to the performance, it was to be a further 20 years before another locomotive (*Woolwinder*) was altered. *C. Lawson Kerr*

2752/60098 *Spion Kop*

Built as 'A3'

Entered traffic	20 April 1929
Renumbered	561 (18 March 1946);
	98 (2 June 1946);
	60098 (3 November 1948)
Liveries	LNER green when new
	Black February 1943
	LNER green March 1947
	BR blue July 1950
	BR green November 1952
Allocations	New to Doncaster
	Haymarket 29 January 1938
	St Margarets
	8 February 1938
	Doncaster 2 March 1938
	Grantham 1 July 1943
	New England 2 April 1944
	King's Cross 18 August 1946
	Haymarket 6 August 1950
	St Margarets 6 January 1963
Withdrawn	28 October 1963;
	to Inverurie Works for
	scrapping, 7 February 1964

Above:
This early picture of *Spion Kop* was taken on 20 May 1933 when it was allocated to Doncaster. It is at the head of the 4pm King's Cross-Newcastle train, passing New Southgate. It changed tenders six times during its career, and at this time was attached to a Great Northern type. Note the fine GNR somersault signals. *E. R. Wethersett*

Above:
During its 13-year stay at Haymarket, *Spion Kop* is shown at Leuchars Junction at the head of the 3.40pm Aberdeen-Edinburgh Waverley service on 14 August 1959, in poor external condition, which was very unusual for Haymarket shed. It is now running with a new-type non-corridor tender and a double chimney, fitted in July 1959, but it never received the trough deflectors. Together with *Felstead*, it was cut up at Inverurie Works. *J. C. Beckett*

2795/60099 Call Boy

Built as 'A3'	
Entered traffic	19 April 1930
Renumbered	99 (21 July 1946);
	E99 (5 March 1948);
	60099 (21 July 1949)
Liveries	LNER green when new
	Black December 1941
	LNER green February 1947
	BR blue July 1949
	BR green July 1952
Allocations	New to Haymarket
	St Margarets 12 January 1940
	Haymarket 19 October 1940
	St Margarets 6 January 1963
Withdrawn	28 October 1963;
	sold to Arnott Young,
	Carmyle, for scrap, June 1964

Above:
Call Boy was an Edinburgh-allocated locomotive for its entire career. When three months old, together with *Spearmint*, it was attached to a corridor tender, and was frequently used on the non-stop 'Flying Scotsman' until 1936, when the tenders were allocated to Class A4s. On 14 September 1934 *Call Boy* races south past Greenwood at the head of the up 'Flying Scotsman'. *E. R. Wethersett*

Below :
Call Boy had only one month left in service when this picture was taken of it arriving at Dundee with a freight from Millerhill on 21 September 1963. Its external condition clearly shows that it did not receive the attention at St Margarets that it had enjoyed at Haymarket over the years. The double chimney was fitted in July 1958, followed by the deflectors in July 1961. *Call Boy* was the only one of the 27 'A3s' built new to have the 'E' prefix to its number 99 in the early nationalisation numbering. *W. S. Sellar*

Right:
Spearmint was probably the most famous of the Haymarket 'A3s' due to being allocated to the well-known driver Norman McKillop of that depot. It changed tenders five times, and is shown here with a Great Northern type at the head of the up 'Queen of Scots' near Burnmouth on 3 August 1951 when it was running in blue livery. *E. R. Wethersett*

2796/60100 *Spearmint*

Built as 'A3'

Entered traffic	17 May 1930
Renumbered	100 (20 July 1946); 60100 (13 April 1949)
Liveries	LNER green when new Black February 1943 LNER green November 1947 BR blue November 1950 BR green September 1952
Allocations	New to Haymarket Aberdeen 4 April 1937 Haymarket 6 March 1938 Eastfield 19 July 1938 Dundee 5 October 1940 Haymarket 14 December 1940 St Margarets 6 January 1963
Withdrawn	19 June 1965; condemned following arrival at Darlington Works for repairs, 31 May 1965

Centre right:
Spearmint received its double chimney in September 1958, and is seen here at the head of the 2.15pm Edinburgh Waverley-Aberdeen train approaching Turnhouse on 26 November 1959. It is now running with a new-type non-corridor tender. *W. S. George*

Left:
Spearmint's last general overhaul was in August 1962, which is probably why it survived to be one of the last three in service. It is seen in its final condition on Gateshead shed on 8 February 1964, with the deflectors that were fitted in August 1961. It also now has a split handrail on the smokebox and the lowered numberplate. *Gavin Morrison*

Above:
Cicero ran with a new-type non-corridor tender for its entire career. It was seldom seen south of Newcastle, and it had short spells at all the Scottish sheds that had 'A3s' allocated, but it is best remembered as a Haymarket engine, where it spent more than 20 years. This is an early picture of the locomotive on the 9.55am Edinburgh-Aberdeen train approaching Kirkcaldy on 26 August 1936. *E. R. Wethersett*

2797/60101 *Cicero*

Built as 'A3'	
Entered traffic	4 June 1930
Renumbered	101 (14 July 1946); 60101 (20 August 1948)
Liveries	LNER green when new Black January 1943 LNER green May 1947 BR blue December 1949 BR green September 1951
Allocations	New to Haymarket Dundee 15 February 1937 Eastfield 20 November 1938 St Margarets 2 February 1940 Haymarket 19 October 1940 St Margarets 6 January 1963
Withdrawn	11 April 1963; sold to Arnott Young, Carmyle, June 1964 for scrap

Left:
Cicero had its last general overhaul in August 1960 when it received the boiler from *Flying Scotsman*. The double chimney was fitted in February 1959, but it never received deflectors. With plenty of coal in the tender it is shown awaiting attention on the out-of-use road at Haymarket, which was parallel to the main line just east of the shed, on 25 August 1962. *Gavin Morrison*

4471/60102 Sir Frederick Banbury

Built new as 'A1'	July 1922; entered traffic as 'A3' 16 October 1942
Renumbered	102 (24 August 1946); 60102 (13 May 1949)
Liveries (as 'A3')	LNER green October 1942 Black October 1942 LNER green January 1947 BR blue May 1949 BR green August 1951
Allocations (as 'A3')	Doncaster 16 October 1942 Grantham 1 July 1943 New England 30 April 1944 Grantham 11 October 1944 Leicester Central 16 May 1949 Neasden 4 July 1952 Leicester Central 21 November 1954 King's Cross 1 September 1957 Doncaster 13 October 1957 Grantham 14 June 1959 King's Cross 9 October 1960
Withdrawn	14 November 1961; to Doncaster Works for scrapping

Upper right:
This is a superb picture of *Sir Frederick Banbury* in LNER apple green but numbered 102. It is at the head of an up express at the southern end of the East Coast main line. The picture is undated but must have been after August 1946, when it received that number.
R. F. Dearden

Centre right:
Sir Frederick Banbury spent more than eight years working trains on the Great Central main line, and is seen here at the head of the up 'Master Cutler' passing Ruddington, in poor external condition.
Ian Allan Library

Lower right:
In its final condition *Sir Frederick Banbury* is awaiting the 'right away' from the guard at Leeds Central at the head of the 12.20pm to King's Cross on 21 April 1961. It received the double chimney in April 1959 during a non-classified repair, and was always attached to a Great Northern-type tender. *Gavin Morrison*

Above:

Flying Scotsman has become internationally famous and the most photographed locomotive in the world. However, its fame was achieved as an 'A1' rather than an 'A3', when it spent most of its time on the southern section of the East Coast main line. This picture shows it running in LNER apple green with the number 103, which it carried between May 1946 and 15 March 1948, when the 'E' prefix was added. It also carried the number 502 from January to March 1946, when it was still an 'A1'. There are no details of the picture, other than the fact that it is an up express during *Flying Scotsman's* time allocated to Doncaster. *R. F. Dearden*

Below:

For nearly 3½ years *Flying Scotsman* was away from its East Coast main line duties, working expresses on the Great Central main line. Here it is seen heading the up 'South Yorkshireman' near Rugby, but no date is given. Like most of the 'A3s' on the Great Central, it was not very clean, and was probably in the BR blue livery. *T. G. Hepburn*

4472/60103 *Flying Scotsman*

Built new as 'A1'	February 1923; entered traffic as 'A3' 4 January 1947
Renumbered	502 (March 1946); 103 (May 1946); E103 (15 March 1948); 60103 (30 December 1948)
Liveries (as 'A3')	LNER green January 1947 BR blue December 1949 BR green March 1952
Allocations (as 'A3')	Doncaster 4 January 1947 Leicester Central 4 June 1950 Grantham 15 November 1953 King's Cross 20 June 1954 Grantham 29 August 1954 King's Cross 7 April 1957
Withdrawn	15 January 1963; sold into preservation, purchased by Alan Pegler

Above:
Flying Scotsman is seen inside the erecting shop at 'The Plant' (Doncaster Works) receiving a casual light repair on 20 March 1960. The double chimney had been fitted in January 1959. *Gavin Morrison*

Below:
Flying Scotsman is in immaculate condition after its last general overhaul at Doncaster, photographed on 8 June 1962 at Wortley South Junction, Leeds, after turning on the triangle to go on to Copley Hill shed for servicing. *Gavin Morrison*

4473/60104 *Solario*

Built new as 'A1'	March 1923; entered traffic as 'A3' 11 October 1941
Renumbered	104 (12 May 1946); 60104 (28 July 1948)
Liveries (as 'A3')	Black October 1941 LNER green January 1947 BR blue December 1949 BR green March 1952
Allocations (as 'A3')	Gorton 11 October 1941 King's Cross 5 February 1943 Leicester Central 4 June 1950 Neasden 4 July 1954 Leicester Central 26 December 1954 King's Cross 1 September 1957 Doncaster 13 October 1957 Grantham 14 June 1959 King's Cross 1 November 1959
Withdrawn	7 December 1959; at Doncaster Works for repair but withdrawn and cut up, December 1959

Above:

It is hard to believe that *Solario* had a general repair and repaint into apple green livery only four months before this picture was taken — obviously Top Shed must have been short of cleaners! It is heading the heavy down 'Aberdonian' (7.30pm from King's Cross) past Finsbury Park on 27 May 1947. *E. R. Wethersett*

Above:

In sharp contrast to the previous picture and taken only five months later, on 6 October 1947, *Solario* is looking immaculate in LNER apple green livery as it heads the up 'Yorkshire Pullman' past Wood Green. It carried the number 104 between 12 May 1946 and 28 July 1948, and became the first 'A3' to be withdrawn, in December 1959. *E. R. Wethersett*

Right:
A fine picture of *Victor Wild* climbing the 1 in 100 out of Leeds Central station at the head of the 3.25pm to King's Cross. Although the picture is not dated, it must have been after September 1951, as the locomotive is carrying a 35B Grantham shedplate. *Eric Treacy*

4474/60105 *Victor Wild*

Built new as 'A1'	March 1923; entered traffic as 'A3' 1 October 1942
Renumbered	105 (12 May 1946); 60105 (18 August 1948)
Liveries	Black October 1942 LNER green May 1947 BR blue March 1950 BR green February 1953
Allocations (as 'A3')	Gorton 1 October 1942 King's Cross 22 November 1942 Grantham 9 September 1951
Withdrawn	16 June 1963; to Doncaster Works for scrapping, 22 August 1963

Centre right:
Having received its double chimney during a general overhaul in March 1959, *Victor Wild* takes the old East Coast main line route via Selby at Chaloners Whin with the up 'Heart of Midlothian' on 18 May 1959. *Gavin Morrison*

Lower right:
Now running with deflectors, which it received during its general overhaul in December 1960, *Victor Wild* climbs towards Stoke Tunnel past Great Ponton at the head of an up express on 7 July 1962. *Gavin Morrison*

Left:
Showing a 37B (Copley Hill) shedplate, *Flying Fox* makes a fine sight at the head of the down 'West Riding' near Marshmoor on 19 August 1955. Note the streamlined articulated stock next to the locomotive. As it was one of the later conversions, it never carried the 'A3' black livery, and entered traffic as No 106 as an A3, retaining that number until 3 December 1948.
E. R. Wethersett

4475/60106 *Flying Fox*

Built new as 'A1'	April 1923; entered traffic as 'A3' 15 March 1947
Renumbered	106 (May 1946); 60106 (3 December 1948)
Liveries (as 'A3')	LNER green March 1947 BR blue May 1950 BR green April 1952
Allocations (as 'A3')	New England 15 March 1947 Grantham 9 November 1947 King's Cross 15 February 1953 Grantham 25 October 1953 Copley Hill 2 May 1954 Leicester Central 28 August 1955 Grantham 15 September 1957 Doncaster 8 September 1963 New England 20 October 963
Withdrawn	26 December 1964; sold to R. A. King, Norwich, for scrap, February 1965

Centre left:
Flying Fox received its double chimney in December 1958, and is on Doncaster shed awaiting a visit to the Works for a casual light repair on 6 November 1960.
Gavin Morrison

Lower left:
Flying Fox received deflectors during a visit to Doncaster in October 1961. It is shown here, away from its usual routes near March South Junction at the head of an up Leeds-King's Cross express, which has been diverted due to a collision at Offord on 8 September 1963. It is worth noting that *Flying Fox* was condemned on Boxing Day 1964, when you would have thought those responsible for taking such decisions would have been on holiday! *B. R. Sheldon*

Right:
Looking very impressive in apple green livery with 'British Railways' on the tender, *Royal Lancer* passes Potters Bar on 14 July 1949 at the head of the down 'Yorkshire Pullman'. Although it ran with the Great Northern-type tender only as an 'A3', it did run with corridor and new-type non-corridor tenders for periods when it was an 'A1'. *E. R. Wethersett*

Below:
Royal Lancer received its double chimney during a casual light repair in June 1959. It is at the head of the 12.30pm Leeds Central to King's Cross train climbing the 1 in 100 to Ardsley Tunnel near Tingley Junction flyover on 11 May 1961.
Gavin Morrison

4476/60107 *Royal Lancer*

Built new as 'A1'	May 1923; entered traffic as 'A3' 4 October 1946
Renumbered	107 (4 October 1946); 60107 (23 April 1948)
Liveries (as 'A3')	LNER green October 1946 BR blue October 1949 BR green December 1952
Allocations (as 'A3')	King's Cross 4 October 1946 Leicester Central 4 June 1950 Copley Hill 27 July 1952 Leicester Central 10 August 1952 Grantham 15 September 1957 King's Cross 9 October 1960 Grantham 16 June 1963
Withdrawn	1 September 1963; to Doncaster Works for scrapping, 4 October 1963

Right:
Royal Lancer was specially groomed to work the 'White Rose' express between King's Cross and Leeds Central in April 1962 to promote the woollen industry. It is leaving Leeds Central on the up working on the 9th with the very distinctive headboard. The Pullman coach in the background is on the 'Queen of Scots'. *Gavin Morrison*

4477/60108 *Gay Crusader*

Built new as 'A1'	June 1923; entered traffic as 'A3' 30 January 1943
Renumbered	507 (28 March 1946); 108 (5 May 1946); 60108 (25 March 1949)
Liveries (as 'A3')	Black January 1943 LNER green August 1947 BR blue September 1950 BR green February 1952
Allocations (as 'A3')	King's Cross 30 January 1943 Doncaster 7 January1951 King's Cross 22 June 1952 Neasden 28 September 1952 King's Cross 29 March 1953 Neasden 29 November 1953 King's Cross 10 July 1955 Neasden 2 October 1955 King's Cross 27 January 1957 Doncaster 19 October 1958 King's Cross 2 November 1958 New England 10 September 1961 Grantham 16 June 1963 Doncaster 8 September 1963
Withdrawn	19 October 1963; to Darlington Works for cutting up, 16 November 1963

Above:
Gay Crusader had received a general overhaul four months before this picture was taken, which included the fitting of the double chimney. It was obviously in excellent condition as on 11 September 1959 it was entrusted with the up 'Flying Scotsman', which unfortunately was not carrying a headboard. It is shown passing Stukeley. *E. R. Wethersett*

Right:
Gay Crusader is only a month away from withdrawal as it waits for its next duty on Doncaster shed on 15 September 1963. The deflectors were fitted in November 1961. *Gavin Morrison*

4478/60109 Hermit

Built new as 'A1'	July 1923; entered traffic as 'A3' 16 November 1943
Renumbered	508 (20 January 1946); 109 (22 June 1946); 60109 (1 May 1948)
Liveries (as 'A3')	Black November 1943 LNER green March 1947 BR blue November 1949 BR green November 1952
Allocations (as 'A3')	Doncaster 16 November 1943 Copley Hill 3 December 1943 New England 29 May 1944 King's Cross 24 September 1944 Grantham 9 September 1951 Doncaster 18 October 1953 King's Cross 8 June 1958 Doncaster 19 October 1958 King's Cross 5 April 1959
Withdrawn	29 December 1962; to Doncaster Works for cutting up, 5 April 1963

Above:
Hermit, in appalling external condition, heads an express through the London suburbs on a heavy train. It is running with the number 109, so the photograph must have been taken between 22 June 1946 and 1 May 1949, when it became No 60109. *Ian Allan Library*

Below:
A fine picture of *Hermit* leaving Retford with an up express during November 1957, when it was allocated to Doncaster. *D. Penney*

4478/60109 *Hermit*

Left:
During a general overhaul in March 1959 *Hermit* received a double chimney, and it is shown here on 17 June 1960 at the head of the down 4.05pm to Leeds and Bradford, ready to leave King's Cross. *D. C. Ovenden*

Below:
Although *Hermit* had only five months to go before withdrawal, it appears to be in fine condition as it takes the slow line at Stoke Summit with the up 'White Rose' to allow the up 'Queen of Scots' to overtake it down Stoke Bank on 21 July 1962. The deflectors were fitted in January 1961 during its last general overhaul.
Gavin Morrison

4479/60110 *Robert The Devil*

Built new as 'A1'	July 1923; entered traffic as 'A3' 8 August 1942
Renumbered	110 (24 August 1946); 60110 (2 March 1949)
Liveries (as 'A3')	Black August 1942 LNER green February 1947 BR blue August 1950 BR green August 1951
Allocations (as 'A3')	New England 8 August 1942 Grantham 11 October 1942 King's Cross 27 October 1946 Grantham 9 September 1951 King's Cross 16 June 1957
Withdrawn	23 May 1963; to Doncaster Works for cutting up, 11 June 1963

Upper right:
Resplendent in LNER apple green livery but numbered 60110 with 'British Railways' on the tender, *Robert The Devil* emerges from Potters Bar North Tunnel at the head of the 4.52pm train from King's Cross to Grantham and Lincoln on 7 May 1949. It was named after the racehorse that won the St Leger in 1880. *E. R. Wethersett*

Centre right
During its entire career of 40 years as an 'A1' and 'A3', *Robert The Devil* was always allocated to the southern sheds on the East Coast main line. While at King's Cross for its last six years, it is at the head of the down 'Yorkshire Pullman' near Woolmer Green on 13 June 1959, having received its double chimney the previous month.
E. R. Wethersett

Lower right:
Having been coaled at York shed, *Robert The Devil* is in the yard ready for its next duty on 13 May 1962, although not in the normal external condition associated with Top Shed. The deflectors were fitted in July 1961, probably by the shed, as the records do not show it as visiting Doncaster Works at this time. *Gavin Morrison*

4480/60111 *Enterprise*

Built new as 'A1'	August 1923; entered traffic as 'A3' 15 July 1927
Renumbered	111 (4 May 1946); 60111 (28 October 1949)
Liveries (as 'A3')	LNER green July 1927 Black February 1943 LNER green November 1947 BR blue October 1949 BR green March 1953
Allocations (as 'A3')	Grantham 15 July 1927 Doncaster 16 July 1927 Carlisle 18 December 1928 King's Cross 5 April 1929 Doncaster 14 April 1929 King's Cross 5 March 1939 Grantham 31 December 1941 Copley Hill 1 October 1943 Grantham 11 October 1943 New England 29 May 1944 Doncaster 12 December 1948 Neasden 20 February 1949 Leicester Central 27 March 1955 Grantham 15 September 1957
Withdrawn	29 December 1962; to Doncaster Works for cutting up, 3 April 1963

Above:
Enterprise was the first 'A1' to be converted to an 'A3' in 1927, and it took 25 years before the last one, *Sir Visto*, was rebuilt in November 1948. This early picture shows *Enterprise* at the head of a down Leeds express, with the locomotive number on the tender. *Ian Allan Library*

Left:
Enterprise now has its number on the cabside, but is still in apple green livery on 12 August 1937 as it heads north at Ganwick on the 4pm from King's Cross. It ran with the Great Northern-type tender until May 1938, then changed to a new-type non-corridor tender for the rest of its career. *E. R. Wethersett*

Right:
Enterprise still has steam to spare as it emerges from Stoke Tunnel with an up express on 21 July 1962. The deflectors were fitted during its last visit to Doncaster Works for a casual repair in April 1962, so it ran with them for only eight months.
Gavin Morrison

As already suggested, 1961 must have been a period when Grantham shed was very short of cleaners. *Enterprise* is seen here leaving Wakefield Westgate on a down King's Cross-Leeds express on 24 August. The double chimney was fitted during a general overhaul in June 1959. *Gavin Morrison*

Left:
Two months before it received its double chimney, *St Simon* is on Doncaster shed on 11 May 1958. Being a late conversion to an 'A3', it did not have the black livery. *Gavin Morrison*

4481/60112 *St Simon*

Built new as 'A1'	September 1923; entered traffic as 'A3' 30 August 1946
Renumbered	112 (May 1946); E112 (20 January 1948); 60112 (25 March 1949)
Liveries (as 'A3')	LNER green August 1946 BR blue February 1951 BR green October 1952
Allocations (as 'A3')	King's Cross 30 August 1946 Copley Hill 4 June 1950 Doncaster 26 November 1950 Copley Hill 1 April 1951 Doncaster 9 September 1951 Grantham 7 October 1951 Doncaster 15 February 1953 Grantham 14 June 1959 Doncaster 8 September 1963 New England 30 October 1963
Withdrawn	26 December 1964; sold to R. A. King, Norwich, for scrap, February 1965

Left:
St Simon was one of the four 'A3s' during British Railways days to receive these winged deflectors, which were of no use, having been tried many years earlier on *Humorist*. Here No 60112 is leaving York past Holgate and blowing off at the head of an up express to King's Cross on 16 June 1962. The double chimney was fitted in July 1958. *Gavin Morrison*

Lower left:
In terrible external condition *St Simon* is on York shed on 2 May 1964, with the trough deflectors that it received in October 1962 during its last general overhaul. It now has a split smokebox handrail and the lowered numberplate. *Gavin Morrison*

Flying Scotsman in preservation

Upper right:

Almost 40 years have passed since the world's most famous locomotive was withdrawn from service. Since that day (15 January 1963) the locomotive has continued in service, with only short breaks, including the problematic trip to the United States. Today it is in regular service, probably in better condition than it ever has been in preservation, and putting up excellent performances. This picture shows it on the Woodhead route back in April 1964 passing Torside on the 'Great Central Rail Tour'. It will be seen from the allocations shown elsewhere in the book that it spent some time allocated to Neasden and Leicester Central working Great Central expresses. *Gavin Morrison*

Centre right:

Flying Scotsman must be the most widely travelled steam locomotive ever built in this country. This picture shows it on the Calder Valley main line passing though Luddendenfoot cutting and heading west with a special on 1 June 1969. Note it is attached to two tenders. *Gavin Morrison*

Below:

Flying Scotsman has probably made more trips over the Settle & Carlisle line than any other preserved locomotive. Here we see it storming across Ribblehead Viaduct, also known as Batty Moss, on the 'Lord Bishop' special on 30 September 1978. *Gavin Morrison*

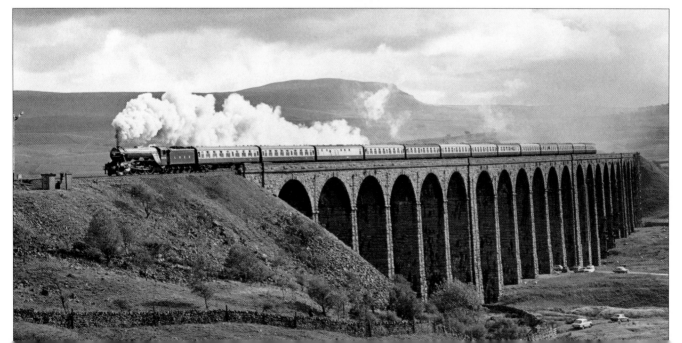

Above:
On 30 January 1983 *Flying Scotsman* was used to haul a special from Carlisle to Garsdale organised by the Steam Locomotive Operators' Association for its Annual General Meeting. It is making rather heavy weather of the climb as it approaches the summit at Ais Gill in the wintry weather. It is attached to the tender from Class A4 *Sir Nigel Gresley* — the stainless steel letters can be clearly seen. *Gavin Morrison*

Left:
Prior to its last major overhaul, *Flying Scotsman* spent some time running on preserved lines in the BR green livery, with double chimney and deflectors. This picture shows it on the Llangollen Railway crossing the Dee Bridge on 19 March 1994. Currently it is still running in this condition, but painted in LNER apple green. *B. Dobbs*